THE BEST BOSTON SPORTS ARGUMENTS

THE 100 MOST CONTROVERSIAL, DEBATABLE QUESTIONS FOR DIE-HARD BOSTON FANS

JIM CAPLE & STEVE BUCKLEY

Published by Sourcebooks, Inc.
P.O. Box 4410, Naperville, Illinois 60567-4410
(630) 961-3900
Fax: (630) 961-2168
www.sourcebooks.com

Library of Congress Cataloging-in-Publication Data

Caple, Jim.
  The best Boston sports arguments : the 100 most controversial, debatable ques-
tions for die-hard Boston fans / James Caple and Stephen Buckley.
      p. cm.
  Includes index.
  1. Sports--Massachusetts--Boston--Miscellanea. I. Buckley, Stephen (Stephen
D.) II. Title.

GV584.5.B6C27 2007
796.0974461--dc22
                                                          2006032392

Printed and bound in the United States of America.
RRD 10 9 8 7 6 5

CONTENTS

INTRODUCTION

On the following pages, you will find the 100 best arguments in Boston sports history.

Which is to say, the only sports arguments that really matter.

We mean, c'mon. Sure, fans are passionate about sports all over the country, but could you get anywhere near as many good, well-rounded sports arguments going in, say, Tampa Bay?

"Who's the greatest Devil Ray in history, Fred McGriff or Randy Winn?"

Or what about Phoenix? How much could winning the World Series in 2001 have really meant to those guys given that they didn't even have a team until 1998? Sure, they had to put up with Buck Showalter and his ego, but what sort of real pain could they have endured in just four seasons?

"Man, remember that one day in 1999 when it was, like, 85 degrees outside and the UV Index was 8.5 and they didn't close the roof?"

That's the beauty of Boston sports. Boston has history. And we're not talking about the "Here's the Granary Burial Ground where founding fathers John Hancock and Samuel Adams are buried" crapola they feed you on the Freedom Trail tour. We're talking about real history. The important stuff. Like, "Here's Fenway Park, where the Sox buried the Yankees in Game 4 in 2004 when Big Papi went deep into a Sam Adams in the right field seats."

Boston also has all four major pro sports, plus enough college sports to drain a booster's secret checking account. Not only that, those sports all have a rich history so long that it even predates the Big Dig.

Boston has the Red Sox, Celtics, Patriots, and Bruins. Boston College and Harvard and Northeastern. The Beanpot and the Marathon. Fenway and the old Garden, the Green Monster and the champion banners hanging from the rafter, "Hail Flutie" and "Havlicek stole the ball!" It not only has city icons, it has some of the biggest icons in sports history --Ted Williams, Bobby Orr, and Bill Russell, plus Tom Brady. (No city can top that quartet. And that's just the first string. What other city has to argue over whether Russell or Larry Bird was its greatest basketball player? Certainly not Denver.)

With a city like this, you could drink the Cask 'n' Flagon dry without settling most of the sports debates. Who's the Best Pitcher in Red Sox history–Roger Clemens, Pedro Martinez, Lefty Grove, or Cy Young? What's the best moment in Boston sports history--winning the 2004 World Series, beating the Yankees in the ALCS, or something else entirely? What was worse, the Bucky Dent home run or the Aaron Boone home run? Who was better, Teddy Ballgame or Joltin' Joe? What was a bigger home run, Pudge's in

Game 6 or Big Papi's in Game 4? What was the most bone-headed move the Red Sox ever made—wait, better hold off on your answer because we're still getting candidates for that one.

And, hell, those are just a couple arguments about one team.

So, why are we wasting your time with this introduction? Get reading! We've got an entire book of arguments about everything from whether Johnny Damon was a traitor (yes) to what was really Orr's biggest goal (hint—you don't have a photo of it mounted on your wall). You probably won't agree with all our conclusions, but that's all right. Disagreement is the nature of a good sports argument, especially in a town like Boston.

Just so long as you're OK with being wrong.

ARE THE GREATEST OF THE GREATS FROM BOSTON?

1 The inspiration for this chapter is a December 6, 1992 must-see event in which Bob Lobel of Boston's WBZ-TV invited three Boston sports icons—Ted Williams, Larry Bird and Bobby Orr—into the station's Soldiers Field Road studios for a live Sunday night chat.

Taken individually, the three legends would not have made for historic television. They had all done their share of television over the years, with Williams, especially, becoming cuddlier, less curmudgeonly, as he grew older.

But this was different. This was an occasion on which three greats from their respective sports were seated alongside each other, admiring one another as thousands at home admired them.

To borrow from Lobel's magical evening of television, let's pose this question: Which North American city has collectively produced the greatest stars in the four major sports leagues?

And the answer, naturally, is Boston . . . or else we wouldn't be writing about it.

THE BEST BOSTON SPORTS ARGUMENTS

From Lobel's interview, we'll take Ted Williams, considered by many to be the greatest hitter that ever lived. And we'll take Bobby Orr, considered by many to be the greatest hockey player of all time. Our choice on the basketball side would be the Celtics' Bill Russell, though Larry Legend will also do nicely.

Football? True, it's too soon to proclaim Patriots quarterback Tom Brady the greatest football player of all time. But the man did quarterback the Patriots to three Super Bowl championships in four years, and, anyway, flattering comparisons between Brady and Joe Montana have been in the books for a couple of years.

Now, put the four of them together. Ted Williams, representing baseball. Bobby Orr, representing hockey. Bill Russell (or Larry Bird) representing basketball. And Tom Brady representing football.

No other city can produce a foursome on par with these men.

There are those out Detroit way who would say, excuse please, Ty Cobb happens to be the greatest hitter of all time. They could also argue, persuasively, the hockey prowess of Gordie Howe. And, yes, the Detroit Lions' Barry Sanders was one of football's great running backs. Alas, there is no stop-the-presses basketball player on this list. No slam dunk, if you will. Dave Bing? Bob Lanier? Isiah Thomas?

Great, yes. Greatest, no.

New York? Babe Ruth is your baseball player. You could go with Lawrence Taylor or Frank Gifford as your football player. Maybe even Y.A. Tittle, or, for those with a flare for the night life, Joe Namath. The region's three NHL clubs offer various Mark Messiers and Bryan Trottiers, Rod Gilberts and Mike Bossys, Denis Potvins and John MacLeans . . . but nobody in Orr's company. Patrick Ewing, Walt Frazier, Earl Monroe, and Willis Reed fall short on the hoops end. But we will take Bill Bradley as the greatest basketball player who ever ran for president.

Los Angeles? You could say Sandy Koufax was the greatest left-handed pitcher of all time, and that Wayne Gretzky, once a King, was/is the greatest of hockey players. Wilt Chamberlain and Kareem Abdul-Jabbar are worthy candidates in basketball. But who's your football player? Eric Dickerson? Let's go with Merlin Olsen, both for his tough, gritty play and his willingness to show us his soft side on "Little House on the Prairie." Which, in the end, disqualifies Los Angeles.

Chicago comes close. Michael Jordan in basketball. Either Bobby Hull or Stan Mikita in hockey. Walter Payton or maybe Gale Sayers in football, not to mention, for you old folks, ol' No. 77 himself, the Galloping Ghost, Red Grange. But two baseball teams, the Cubs and White Sox, have not produced truly great players, though Ernie Banks, Billy Williams, and Luis Aparicio are close.

Too bad Shoeless Joe Jackson didn't get caught up in fixing the 1919 World Series, or he'd be our Chicago baseball representative.

Which brings us back to Boston. Case closed.

WHO IS BOSTON'S GREATEST ATHLETE OF ALL TIME?

2 Re-read the previous chapter and take yet another look at those names. Ted Williams. Bobby Orr. Tom Brady. Larry Bird. Bill Russell.

If you want to round out the cast a little, we'll add Bob Cousy and John Havlicek from the Celtics. Baseball representatives include Cy Young, Pedro Martinez, and Roger Clemens, all of whom have been labeled the greatest pitcher of all time. And don't forget Warren Spahn, who broke into the big leagues with the Boston Braves: You'll find a lot of people who'll explain to you why Spahnie is the greatest left-hander of all time.

Don't forget, too, that Babe Ruth was already considered baseball's best player when he was still with the Red Sox.

Or that the cover of the August 31, 1981 edition of *Sports Illustrated* proclaimed the Patriots' John Hannah as "The Greatest Offensive Lineman of All Time."

Or that a Boston original from another era, John L. Sullivan, born in Roxbury, interred at Roslindale's Mount Calvary Cemetery, used to boast, "I can lick any man in the house." And, for many years, in many houses, did just that.

It's difficult, then, to choose Boston's greatest athlete of all time. It's not like we're making picks for which there can be no discussion, such as the best of The Three Stooges (Curly), or where in Greater Boston to get the best burger (O'Sullivan's, Beacon Street, Somerville.)

Boston's greatest athlete? In the end, it's Bill Russell of the Celtics.

This decision was not easily reached. Boston sports experts were consulted, with the likes of Gerry Callahan of the *Boston Herald*, Bob Ryan of the *Boston Globe*, Bob Lobel of WBZ-TV, Glenn Ordway of WEEI-AM and Dick Johnson of the Sports Museum of New England weighing in.

Lobel went with Orr, because, he said, "the guy revolutionized hockey." Dick Johnson, too, chose Orr: "He was the greatest pure talent I ever saw," he said. "And he's all the more spectacular when you consider what he did playing at 80 percent most of his career because of his bad knees."

Callahan went with Bird, explaining his decision this way: "There was just nobody better than Number—33. If you were a Celtics fan during that time, Bird made it so you could be cocky and confident."

Ryan, as is his style, minced no words: "11 championships."

He's right. During a stretch of 13 seasons, from 1956-57 to 1968-69, the Celtics won 11 National Basketball Association championships. And it so happens that Russell's NBA career lasted 13 seasons—from 1956-57 to 1968-69.

The man was a champion, the greatest Boston has ever known. (OK, heavyweight Rocky Marciano went undefeated, but he was from Brockton, some 20 miles south of Boston.)

Russell was not a Mr. October (or Mr. April, in this case) who ratcheted up his game come playoff time. From start to finish, regular season to postseason, his play was remarkably consistent. He averaged 15.1 points per game in the regular season, 16.2 in the playoffs. He shot 44 percent during the regular season, 43 percent in the playoffs. Even his free-throw percentage, never a strong part of Russell's game, was at least consistent: 56 percent in the regular season, 60 percent in the postseason.

He made a career out of winning the big showdowns against Wilt Chamberlain. He made a career out of winning, period. He even emerged as player-coach at the end of his career, guiding the Celtics to two championships.

In a city with an obsession for winning, it's illogical for anyone other than Bill Russell to be Boston's greatest athlete.

IS JOHNNY DAMON A TRAITOR?

3 In 1951, the United States government tried and convicted Brooklyn residents Julius and Ethel Rosenberg on charges of espionage and passing along atomic bomb secrets to the Soviet Union. Despite an appeal for leniency from the Pope, the two were executed as Soviet spies two years later.

Our country's most controversial case of treason, however, occured in December 2005 when Johnny Damon signed a four-year, $52 million contract with the Yankees.

Should Red Sox fans consider Johnny a traitor? Let's look at the facts. Damon played four seasons with the Red Sox, batting .295 and averaging 115 runs and 25 stolen bases. He made two All-Star teams, helped the Sox to three consecutive postseason appearances, suffered a concussion fighting to keep his club alive in the 2003 postseason, hit a decisive grand slam to spark Boston's Game 7 victory in the 2004 ALCS and played a crucial part in the team finally ending an 86-year, generation-crushing World Series championship drought. In what was likely his last chance for a big payday on the free agent market, he then accepted a contract that was 20 percent higher than the best offer from the Red Sox.

11

On the other hand, he took money from George Steinbrenner.

Forget about the "WWJD?" bumper stickers. The better shorthand is WWJDISBWHA?—What Would Jesus Do If Scott Boras Was His Agent?

Then the Devil took Jesus to a very high mountain and showed him all the kingdoms of the world in all their greatness. "All this I will give you," the Devil said, "if you kneel down and worship me." Then Jesus answered, "Go away, Satan! The scripture says, 'Worship the Lord your God and serve only him!'"

But then Scott Boras whispered, "Let's not be hasty. What if we could get him to guarantee a fifth year, a private plane to fly your family around on road trips, your own merchandising tent at spring training and a $50,000 incentive for every leper you cure?"

And then the Devil replied, "But he'll have to get a haircut and a shave."

Look, this is America, a nation built on capitalism, so no one should fault any player for deciding to take the money and run. But there are exceptions, and Damon signing with the Yankees was an unforgivable act almost as offensive as his cameo appearance in *Fever Pitch*. Fans accept that baseball is a business and a player has to do what makes financial sense. But while you can sign as a free agent with almost any team, you simply do not switch to the sworn enemy. Damon himself acknowledged this in advance the previous May, when he told reporters he could never sign with the Yankees.

It's understandable that the Yankees' offer would turn his head for a moment or two but he should have responded the way Jimmy Stewart does in *It's a Wonderful Life* when Mr. Potter offers him a three-year deal to leave the Bailey Brothers Building and Loan. He initially considers the offer until he shakes hands with Potter. Then he distastefully wipes away Potter's touch from his palm and tells him "In the whole vast configuration of things, you're nothing but a scurvy spider." (Indeed, Lionel Barrymore's performance as Potter eerily evokes Steinbrenner.)

Will Boston view Damon as the lovable idiot who helped the Sox to the 2004 world championship, or the greedy traitor who jumped ship to the Yankees? "There have been many books written, and they're always going to say in 2004 the Red Sox were World Champions," Damon told reporters when he returned to Fenway Park for the first time as a Yankee. "My time here is always going to be remembered for that."

That may be true. Eventually. But baseball is a fickle game. One day you're kneeling down and bowing before a player, the next you're kneeling down and slashing his tires. Plus, few people remember Benedict Arnold for helping win the Battle of Saratoga. So for the moment we'll remember that Damon looked like Jesus, threw like Mary, and acted like Judas.

SHOULD TOM YAWKEY BE ENSHRINED IN BASEBALL'S HALL OF FAME?

4 Like all plaques dedicated to inductees at baseball's Hall of Fame, Thomas A. Yawkey's is short and to the point. It relates that Yawkey gave "more than four decades of dedicated service as owner-president of the Boston Red Sox," notes that he was "rated one of the sport's finest benefactors," and even informs visitors to the Cooperstown baseball shrine that he "set precedent for A.L. in 1936 as first to have team travel by plane."

And those are wonderful bouquets for Yawkey, who owned the Red Sox from 1933 until his death in 1976. But while it's nice to read that Yawkey was ahead of his time in recognizing the importance of air travel, he wasn't much of a trailblazer in other fields.

Take, for instance, racial equality. Though the Brooklyn Dodgers smashed baseball's color line by promoting Jackie Robinson to the big leagues in 1947, it was not until 1959—12 years later—that the Red Sox got around to adding an African American to their roster by promoting Elijah J. "Pumpsie" Green from the team's Minneapolis farm club.

The sad reality is that the Red Sox had a sorry track record in race relations throughout—and even beyond—Yawkey's tenure. The team did yield to public pressure in April 1945 by staging a so-called "tryout" to Robinson, Sam Jethroe, and Marvin Williams, all three of them Negro League stars of the day, but the event was a sham. The three players were never contacted by the Red Sox again, with Robinson going on to a Hall of Fame career with the Dodgers and Jethroe re-emerging in Boston in 1950 as National League Rookie of the Year with the old Boston Braves.

Even if Major League Baseball's Veterans Committee chose to ignore Yawkey's murky past in matters of race, it boggles the mind as to how it could be overlooked that the man's "more than four decades of dedicated service" never resulted in a World Series championship for the Red Sox. The Red Sox won just three American League pennants during the Tom Yawkey era (1946, 1967, 1975), losing Game 7 of the World Series on each occasion.

As if to make up for this, the writers of Yawkey's Hall of Fame plaque dutifully report that the Red Sox "narrowly missed" the postseason in 1948, 1949 and 1972.

So there you have it: The last owner in baseball to integrate . . . a man with no World Series championships during his four-plus decades in the game . . . and a collection of historic near-misses . . . gets into Cooperstown.

Keepers of the Yawkey flame are quick to point out that the man donated millions of dollars to charity, notably the Jimmy Fund, the fundraising arm of Boston's acclaimed Dana-Farber Cancer Institute. Then again, the Yawkey Foundation, formed in 1976 after Yawkey's death, has given boatloads of money to baseball's Hall of Fame.

That might explain why Yawkey is enshrined in Cooperstown, and why Jake Ruppert, who built Yankee Stadium, purchased Babe Ruth from the Red Sox, and lived to see his team win seven World Series championships, is not.

SHOULD BOSTON REPLACE ANCIENT FENWAY PARK?

5 What, are you kidding? Would you tear down the Old North Church to make room for a parking lot? Would you take a wrecking ball to the Old South Meeting Hall to build another Starbucks? Would you scuttle the U.S.S. Constitution for hardwood flooring? Of course not. Those sites are an integral part of our heritage.

So why do so many people want to replace Fenway Park?

Yeah, yeah, we know. Fenway is old, cramped, and uncomfortable. The seats, built for 1912 bodies, are so small there isn't enough leg room for Pedro Martinez's old friend, Nelson de la Rosa. The capacity, more or less capped under 40,000 unless they build seats on top of the Citgo sign, means ticket prices and demand remain so high that pretty much the only people who can afford seats are the players. The facilities are so antiquated that the true Boston Marathon is waiting in line between innings for either a beer or the bathroom. And yes, its dimensions doomed generations of teams built to win at Fenway and destined to lose in October.

So what?

In a city famous for its historic sites, Fenway is Boston's personal Way-Back Machine, transporting fans to the days when our grandparents and great-grandparents were young and bitching about the team not winning a World Series for five whole years. Other cities build new retro-parks that attempt to conjure the past, but Fenway *is* the past. Stepping inside is like stepping into the world's best museum, only instead of dinosaur bones and stuffed blue whales, there was David Wells. You can practically smell the Babe's beer breath.

The oldest ballpark in the majors, this is where Ruth pitched, Ted Williams batted, and Carlton Fisk danced down the baseline. Where Curt Schilling turned the Red Sox into winners, Big Papi turned cynical fans into believers, and Pedro Martinez turned Don Zimmer upside down. Where, like Kevin Costner and James Earl Jones in *Field of Dreams,* you can sit in the stands and feel connected to nearly a century of baseball.

Fenway is living Boston history. You don't get rid of something like this any more than you would paint the Green Monster pink or open a Yankees team store on Landsdowne Street.

The previous ownership group spent a lot of needless time and energy insisting that Fenway was falling apart and needed to be replaced, effort that would have been better spent keeping Roger Clemens on the payroll. Fortunately, the current owners realize that Fenway is a jewel that should be treasured, not condemned. Rather than gripe about Fenway's drawbacks, they made the most of its assets, turning it into even more of a shrine than ever before. They added the seats atop the Green Monster, making them the most coveted tickets in baseball. They added seats on the right field roof as well, and greatly expanded the concession areas throughout the park. And best of all, they added a world championship banner to fly over it all.

Sure, you can remodel Fenway, but replace it? Never. As long as the Red Sox exist, this is the only diamond they should call home.

So if you don't like the cramped seats, tough. Suck in your gut, diet, and leave Fenway alone.

WHAT IS THE MOST UNDERRATED SPORTS VENUE IN BOSTON SPORTS HISTORY?

6 It used to be said you didn't attend football games at Foxboro Stadium, you endured them. Part of this, naturally, is because for too many years the quality of play by the clumsy hometown Patriots was a notch or 12 below that being exhibited by their opponents. But there was also the issue of Foxboro Stadium itself, which was behind the times from the very day it slid off its blueprints and into reality.

Opened in 1970 as Schaefer Stadium and known variously over the years as Sullivan Stadium and, ultimately, Foxboro Stadium, the place was little more than a glorified high school park, a sea of backless aluminum benches with a dank, Spartan underbelly of beer stands and cramped, odious restrooms.

And those were Foxboro's good qualities. But while everyone understands that Foxboro Stadium was never much in the looks department, and that it delivered little in the way of comfort or amenities, it will forever be remembered—that is, it should forever be remembered—as the stadium that saved professional football in New England.

Let's remember, first, that the Patriots were virtually homeless during their first 10 years of existence. They were vagabonds, gridiron wanderers, playing their home games everywhere from Boston University Field (which, essentially, was what remained of old Braves Field) and Fenway Park to Harvard Stadium and Boston College's Alumni Stadium. On September 22, 1968, the Pats even played a "home" game in Birmingham, Alabama.

Once the old American Football League merged with the National Football League, it was obvious the Patriots would need their own stadium to survive. Dozens of plans had been hatched over the years—some of them just pipe dreams, some of them serious enough to merit a press conference and the ever-handy artist's rendition—but what finally materialized was a simple, no-frills stadium located on Route 1 in the town of Foxborough, some 26 miles south of Boston.

Construction began in late 1970, and soon a local beer company, Schaefer, bought the naming rights. Schaefer Stadium opened on August 15, 1971, with 60,423 fans turning out to see the Patriots defeat the New York Giants 20-14 in an exhibition game.

In 1982, the stadium was renamed Sullivan Stadium in honor of William H. "Billy" Sullivan Jr., the onetime public relations director of the old Boston Braves baseball team who in 1959 had headed up the Patriots' original ownership group. After the Sullivan family sold the team, the

Pats' home field was renamed Foxboro Stadium.

The place never had the rich history and the poetry of Fenway Park. It didn't have the urban grittiness of the original Boston Garden, whose primary tenants, the Celtics and Bruins, brought many championships to the old building.

But neither Fenway Park nor Boston Garden saved a major-league sports franchise from exiting the region. And Foxboro Stadium did manage, on its last day of business, to deliver a never-to-be-forgotten moment: The Snow Game. On January 19, 2002, the Pats emerged with a 16-13 overtime playoff victory over the Oakland Raiders, with Adam Vinatieri's 45-yard field goal in the final seconds sending the game into overtime. Vinatieri won the game with a 23-yard field goal; two weeks later, with Foxboro Stadium headed for demolition, the Pats won their first Super Bowl.

WAS IT THE CURSE—OR BIGOTRY—THAT KEPT THE RED SOX FROM OVERTAKING THE YANKEES?

7 The media loved to write about the Curse of the Bambino preventing the Red Sox from winning the World Series for 86 years. But really, it had nothing to do with a Ruth hex and much to do with the organization's bigotry.

The Red Sox infamously were the last baseball team to integrate, waiting 12 years between Jackie Robinson's debut with the Dodgers in 1947 and Pumpsie Green's with Boston in 1959. Hell, even the Bruins integrated before the Red Sox. Black and Latin players won eight MVPs, nine Rookie of the Year awards, five home run crowns, three batting titles, and a Cy Young in those dozen years while the Red Sox roster still was so white you could have taped an episode of *Friends* inside their clubhouse.

This not only was morally indefensible, it was a wasted opportunity from a competitive standpoint. That's because the Yankees were playing Strom Thurmond to Boston's Bull

Connor. The Yankees didn't integrate their roster until 1955, and in the early '60s Elston Howard still was often the only African American in the lineup. Had the Red Sox been as progressive as Cleveland (which had eventual Hall of Famer Larry Doby in its outfield less than three months after Robinson's first game) instead of stubbornly waiting for the baseball equivalent of a Judge Garrity ruling, they might have won the 1948 pennant by four games instead of losing to the Indians in that playoff. And more importantly, they would have been in position to end the Yankees reign. The Red Sox won 286 games from 1948 to 1950 and finished a combined six games out of first place. Think a player the caliber of Roy Campanella or Satchel Paige might have meant the difference of six games over three years? The Red Sox also could have ended the alleged Curse of the Bambino four decades before Dan Shaughnessy popularized the term.

The saddest part is that Boston had the perfect chance to do so in 1945. The Red Sox held a tryout for Robinson, Sam Jethroe, and Marvin Williams, but in their shrewd judgment team executives passed on all three.

Sorry, Mr. Robinson. We're just not sure you have the talent or the character to replace the immortal Catfish Metkovich on our roster.

As if that wasn't bad enough, they also missed on Willie Mays when he played for the Birmingham Black Barons. There are conflicting stories about whether the Red Sox ever scouted Mays, but it's even worse if they didn't. That's because one of their top minor league teams was the Birmingham Barons, who just happened to share the same stadium with Mays' Black Barons.

"My argument is (racism) killed them yesterday and it killed them today," says Howard Bryant, author of *Shut Out*, the splendid book on Red Sox racism. "They passed on Billy Williams. They passed on Mays and more players you can count on. A team with an outfield of Williams and Mays and Aaron, or a team with Robinson and Williams and Mays in the lineup? Yeah, I think their fortunes would have been different...

"What gives racism a face is the Red Sox didn't want to deal with African Americans for so long and it became so much a part of their reputation that as soon as players had control over where they wanted to play, Boston was the last place they would play."

If you think it wasn't a long-term problem, try naming a big-time African American free agent the Red Sox signed prior to Andre Dawson in 1993. "Think how damaging it is for a team trying to win when all-star players have it written into their contract they can't be traded to them," Bryant says, citing Gary Sheffield and David Justice as a few examples.

How would Red Sox history be different had the team been quicker to integrate? Just imagine what the Celtics history would be had they not signed Bill Russell.

WHY JIM RICE'S BEST FRIENDS ARE THE BOSTON BASEBALL WRITERS

8 The conventional wisdom would lead you to believe Jim Rice has been denied access to baseball's Hall of Fame for no other reason than because he was historically mean and surly in his dealings with Boston's cantankerous baseball writers.

It's been said, and written, over and over: "Just because Rice didn't kiss the asses of those Boston sportswriters, they're keeping him out of Cooperstown."

The conventional wisdom is wrong. Oh, to be sure: Jim Rice was mean and surly in his dealings with the writers, who, while we're at it, are every bit as cantankerous as advertised.

But the argument that Boston-based members of the Baseball Writers Association of America are aiming some journalistic payback at the onetime slugger by denying him their Hall of Fame votes . . . well, it's simply not true. An informal poll of Hall of Fame voters representing the Boston chapter of the BBWAA reveals that, over the years, practically all of them have granted Favorite Son status to their not-so-favorite slugger. Rice remains locked out of Cooperstown not because he lacks votes on his home turf, but because he hasn't mustered sufficient support from voters in Cleveland, St. Louis, Detroit, and other big-league ports of call.

The closest Rice has come to being enshrined in Cooperstown was in 2005, when he received 307 votes, or 59.50 percent of the total votes cast. A player must be named on 75 percent of votes cast to be inducted into the Hall of Fame. Given the industrywide backlash against the steroid abusers who polluted the game over the last couple of decades, it was thought that Rice, who played for the Red Sox from 1974 to 1989, would be rewarded for putting up impressive numbers in the pre-juice era. He was "clean," went the chorus from those who believed Rice was headed for Cooperstown. Instead, he picked up just 31 additional votes from the 276 he received in 2004.

Now then: Does Jim Rice belong in Cooperstown? Yes. As was first pointed out by ESPN.com's Jayson Stark, Rice led the American League in home runs, runs batted in, runs, slugging percentage, and extra-base hits from 1975 through 1985, and he was also an eight-time All-Star. He put up the necessary numbers to satisfy a famous Hall of Fame catch phrase: He dominated his era.

Rice's absence from the Hall of Fame is not due to the lack of outstanding seasons. His real problem is that he didn't have a sufficient number of mediocre seasons. Had Rice managed to hang on for four additional seasons in which he averaged, say, .270 with 20 home runs and 75 RBI, he probably would have been given his passage to Cooperstown years ago.

Look at it another way: It took Rice 16 seasons to amass 382 home runs and 1,451 RBI. Tony Perez, meanwhile, played 23 seasons in the big leagues, yet had fewer home runs (379) and only 201 more runs batted in. And Perez was just a .279 career hitter, whereas Rice hit .298.

But, then, you already know all this if you're a Boston baseball writer.

SHOULD DOUG MIENTKIEWICZ HAVE KEPT THE 2004 WORLD SERIES BASEBALL?

9 One problem with going more than eight decades between world championships is that people tend to overreact when you finally do win. Case in point: The debate over who "owned" the baseball Doug Mientkiewicz caught for the final putout of the 2004 World Series.

Mientkiewicz, who had 27 hits for the Red Sox during his three-month Boston career (counting the postseason), was playing first base in the Game 4 clincher when closer Keith

Foulke fielded a ground ball from Edgar Renteria in the bottom of the ninth inning. Foulke tossed the ball to Mientkiewicz, who recorded the force out that wrapped up the championship. Mientkiewicz joked that he put "the Polish death grip" on the ball, then took it home for posterity.

That should have been the end of it, but the Red Sox went over the top with their celebrations and demanded that Mientkiewicz return the ball so they could put it on display. They argued that because he caught the ball while under their employ, it was their property. Upset with the way team president Larry Lucchino went about publicly pressuring him, Mientkiewicz insisted the ball belonged to him, citing the well-established legal doctrine of "Finders keepers, losers weepers." After more than a year of arguments and headlines, the two sides eventually agreed to put the ball in the Hall of Fame (which Mientkiewicz says was always his intent).

"It got to be ridiculous. I turned on CNN and I'm sandwiched between the tsunami and the Laci Peterson murder trial," Mientkiewicz says. "I had people tailing me and my family. I got death threats. Guys were threatening my wife. 'I know what Jodi is wearing—I just saw her in the store.'

"They acted like I went into Fenway and cut the Monster down and moved it away from everybody."

Mientkiewicz is right. The Red Sox did overreact. Did the Mets ever claim that the Buckner ball, which was eventually sold to Charlie Sheen for $93,000, was theirs? Who knows the final location of the Yaz popup ball that Graig Nettles caught to end the 1978 playoff game? Would anyone anywhere want the ball that ended the 1995 Division Series?

Mientkiewicz certainly had precedent on his side for keeping the ball. Teams always allow players to retrieve and keep baseballs that are historic or personally memorable. In the case of base hits or wins, the balls are returned to the dugout for safe keeping. In the case of home runs, employees are dispatched to the stands to help negotiate with the fan who caught the ball. It was petty for the Red Sox to suddenly claim Mientkiewicz wasn't entitled to such a souvenir.

Who really owns a historic baseball? This is the sort of important question Supreme Court justices should be asked during confirmation hearings:

SEN. JOE BIDEN: The Red Sox pay for each item of equipment they provide for the players. Doesn't that give them legal ownership?

JOHN ROBERTS: Let me answer this way. I can go to Wal-Mart and purchase a baseball for $7.99 and that's all it will ever be worth. It's the player who conveys a value to the baseball, not the team that bought it. Furthermore, teams give away baseballs all the time in the form of foul balls hit into the stands. For them to claim a right to keep one just because it has an alleged "value" is inconsistent with their stated policy. More importantly, the Red Sox do not have legal standing. The home team provides the baseballs for each game, and the St. Louis Cardinals were the home team for Game 4, not the Red Sox.

BIDEN: Sounds good to me. All in favor of a Chief Justice Roberts, say 'Aye.'

ENTIRE SENATE: Aye!

SEN. KENNEDY: Great. Now, let's go get some drinks.

Mientkiewicz should have been allowed to keep the ball. It was his. The world championship trophy and pennant, however, were definitely all Boston's.

WHY THE RED SOX HAVE THE DUMBEST RETIRED-NUMBER POLICY IN SPORTS HISTORY

For the sheer comedy of it all, nothing beats going on a tour of Fenway Park with one of those eager-to-please college kids-turned-guides who are thrilled to have what, to them, is the greatest summer job on earth.

And for the most part, these Fenway tour guides know their stuff. They'll tell you all about the Pesky Pole and the Monster and the famous "red seat" in the right field bleachers where Ted Williams once deposited a home run.

But, inevitably, the tour guides must talk about the Red Sox' retired uniform numbers that are displayed on the facing of the right-field roof. That's when they start sounding like tongue-tied defense contractors who have been dragged before a Senate investigative committee.

The easy part is pointing out which numbers have been retired by the Red Sox: Ted Williams (9), Joe Cronin (4), Bobby Doerr (1), Carl Yastrzemski (8), and Carlton Fisk (27).

And then they explain the team's implausible, contradictory "policy" regarding retired uniform numbers. What they should be saying is, "I don't recall, Senator."

Here's the problem. In addition to a) being elected to the Hall of Fame, and b) having played 10 years with the Red Sox, a player must c) "finish his career with the club."

This is when the savvy Fenway tourist says, "But wait a minute, Mr. Tour Guide, didn't Carlton Fisk end his career with the Chicago White Sox?"

True: Fisk, who left the Red Sox after the 1980 season, played the remaining 13 years of his career with the Chisox.

"Yes," says the befuddled tour guide, reading from his dog-eared, team-issued script, "but, you see, Carlton Fisk came back to work for the Red Sox as special assistant to general manager Dan Duquette. So, you see, he really did, um, you know, finish his career with the Red Sox."

Well, no, he did not. It's just the Red Sox wanted to glom onto Fisk after the catcher was elected to the Hall of Fame in 2000. But rather than alter their policy, they simply created a fake job for Fisk and then hoped nobody would notice.

People noticed. Not only did Fisk's fabricated job violate the spirit of their own club policy, the Red Sox also made Ted Williams and Bobby Doerr technically ineligible to have their numbers retired. For if it's true that Fisk "ended his career" with the Red Sox because of his position as "special assistant to the general manager," then Ted Williams "ended his career" as manager of the Texas Rangers in 1972.

The Red Sox would counter that, au contraire, Williams was named a team "consultant" in 1978. But what about Bobby Doerr? The great second baseman ended his career as a coach with the Toronto Blue Jays in 1981, but has never popped up anywhere as an official Red Sox "consultant."

Understand that all of these Red Sox legends, and this includes Carlton Fisk, deserve to have their numbers retired. But they deserve the honor because they were truly great players, not because their respective careers fit snugly within the confines of a contrived team policy.

WHICH YANKEES LOSS WAS MORE PAINFUL, BUCKY DENT OR AARON BOONE?

11 This question is like asking which do you think hurts more, having someone whack the claw end of a hammer into your right eye socket or taking the business end of a garden hoe to your groin? No reasonable person would choose either (though both may be preferable to being stuck in the elevator with an over-the-top Yankees fan).

When the Red Sox won the 2004 World Series, thousands listened to the victory on the radio, not just because they didn't want to hear Tim McCarver but because their shattered TV screens still hadn't been repaired since kicking them in when Aaron Boone took Tim Wakefield deep. That painful home run came at a time when the Red Sox-Yankees rivalry had been whipped into an almost unprecedented furor by the continuing dominance of the Yankees and the spirited violence of the Pedro-Zimmer game.

The loss was excruciating, because you saw it coming but couldn't do a damn thing to stop it. Even when the Red Sox took a 4-0 lead and Pedro was dealing from the mound, you just knew it would somehow end horribly. And sure enough it did. Pedro tired and Grady Little left him in. Pedro grew more tired and his release point dropped and his pitches rose in the strike zone and Grady still left him in. Pedro grew more tired and his shoulder began smoking and his elbow began making the type of sounds seldom heard outside a dentist's office and Grady walked slowly to the mound, talked it over with his pitcher and then inexplicably left him in to face left-handed-hitting Hideki Matsui. Naturally, Matsui doubled. And Grady still left Pedro in to give up a game-tying single.

The charitable thing for the Red Sox would have been to lose the lead and the game right then and there. Instead, second baseman Todd Walker made a spectacular diving stop to preserve the tie and prolong the agony several more innings. Boone finally put an end to it all when he homered off Wakefield in the 11th inning.

Yes, that was a pretty miserable game. But the Bucky Dent 1978 playoff loss was even more painful.

Why? Because unlike the 2003 Red Sox, the 1978 Sox had the division title wrapped up by mid-season. They clearly were the best team in baseball. They had the game's best hitter, Jim Rice, having the best season of his career. They had Yaz and Pudge and Dewey and the Eck. They had a 14-game lead over the Yankees in July. There was no way even the Red Sox could blow a lead like that. And then they did, watching it ebb away; slowly at first, and then with a rush during the infamous Boston Massacre in September, when the Yankees outscored them 46-9 while the Sox made 11 errors in four games. More than anything, this is the season that cemented Boston's reputation of always failing in the clutch.

And like the 2003 Red Sox, the '78 team wouldn't let it end there. They rallied with two superb final weeks to tie New York and force the one-game playoff at home. They took an early lead in that game only to watch it and their hopes disappear into the net with Dent's home run.

The question haunting fans after 2003 was whether things might have been different had Grady taken Pedro out earlier. There were many what-ifs to torment Sox fans after 1978. What if Zimmer hadn't blown out his pitching staff during the season? What if Lou Piniella had not positioned himself directly in the path of Fred Lynn's line drive in the playoff? What if the wind hadn't switched direction for Dent's at-bat?

Furthermore, as painful as the 2003 loss was at the time, the pain only lasted a year. The Red Sox healed all by beating the Yankees in the 2004 ALCS. The 1978 loss, however, had a quarter-century to fester, grow infected, and create an ugly, painful scab that we just couldn't stop ourselves from picking at amid memories of that Bucky #@#% Dent and his @#$% home run . . . .

You'll have to excuse us for a minute now while we try to calm down.

SHOULD TONY CONIGLIARO'S NO. 25 BE RETIRED?

12 Scroll through the list of retired uniform numbers of various big-league baseball teams and you'll occasionally come across a player who was honored not so much for his statistics as for the intangibles that can only be understood and appreciated by the hometown fans.

Jim Umbricht's No. 32 was retired by the old Houston Colt 45's (now the Houston Astros) in 1964, after he'd lost a courageous battle with cancer. Jimmie Reese, who spent most of his playing career in the Pacific Coast League, had a brief fling with the New York Yankees (with whom he famously roomed with Babe Ruth) and later became a much-loved coach with the California Angels, wore No. 50—retired by the club following his death in 1994 at age 92. And in 1987, after Kansas City Royals manager Dick Howser succumbed to a brain tumor, the club did the right thing and retired his No. 10.

None of these players is in the Hall of Fame, but they contributed much more than "numbers" to their respective ballclubs. It is in this spirit that the Boston Red Sox should abandon their absurd "policy" as pertains to these matters and retire the No. 25 that Tony C. wore during his years with the club.

A native of the Boston area and a onetime schoolboy phenom at St. Mary's High School in nearby Lynn, Conigliaro was just 19 when, in 1964, he made his major-league debut with the Red Sox. In 1965, at the age of 20, he became the youngest player to lead the American League in home runs, with 32. He would later become the second-youngest player in history to amass 100 career home runs.

Conigliaro's career was derailed on an August night in 1967, when he was hit in the left eye by a pitch thrown by Angels pitcher Jack Hamilton. He would miss the remainder of the Sox' 1967 "Impossible Dream" season, and all of 1968, but he made an emotional, never-to-be-forgotten return to the club in 1969, hitting 20 home runs. The next year, after hitting 36 home runs and knocking in 116 runs, he was traded, curiously, to the Angels.

His eyesight failing him, he retired from baseball in 1971, but in 1975 made yet another comeback with the Red Sox, this time as a designated hitter. He made the club out of spring training and was in the Opening Day lineup. He received a thunderous ovation, as did the game's all-time home run king, Henry Aaron, who was making his American League debut with the Milwaukee Brewers.

This last comeback stalled in the late spring, and Conigliaro retired yet again, this time for good. But he waged

37

one final battle—for his life. In 1982, after auditioning for a role as color analyst with the Red Sox' television network, he suffered a crippling heart attack while being driven to Logan Airport by his brother, former Sox outfielder Billy Conigliaro. He never recovered, and spent his remaining years being cared for by his family; he died in 1990.

Had he not been beaned on that night in 1967, Conigliaro was on his way to becoming one of the game's all-time home run kings. Given his powerful right-handed swing, magnificently crafted for Fenway Park, he might have hit 600 home runs.

But more than all that, Tony Conigliaro, then and now, stands as proof that a local kid can grow up and become a star with the hometown team. He was, and remains, the quintessential comeback kid.

That the Red Sox have not retired his uniform number is itself a tragedy.

IF YOU COULD GO TO ANY GAME IN BOSTON HISTORY, WHICH SHOULD YOU CHOOSE?

13 Say you're rubbing your bottle of Sam Adams one night at the Cask'n' Flagon and a magic genie suddenly appears and offers to grant you three wishes. So after the genie transfers Bill Gates' money into your bank account and deposits Angelina Jolie in your bed, you're left with one wish for anything you want to do. Do you cure cancer? End worldwide poverty and hunger? Establish peace in the Middle East?

No. You use that wish on something wise—like seeing one game from any era in Boston history.

Which one would you choose? Game 4 of the 2004 ALCS? Game 5? Game 6 of the 1975 World Series? Super Bowl XXXVI? The 1984 Boston College-Miami football game? Game 7 of the 1965 Eastern Conference Finals?

There's nothing wrong with any of those choices. But there's no big deal seeing them again, either, given that they're available on tape and you can pretty much watch or listen to them anytime you want.

But here's a game unavailable on any tape or film reel, a game that offers perhaps the most extraordinary display in baseball history—with the possible exception of Oscar Gamble's afro.

Red Sox vs. Senators, June 23, 1917.

Granted, not exactly a date that lives in infamy, but here's what you get for your ticket.

You get to see Fenway Park when it was just five years old, when Duffy's Cliff was in left field, but no Green Monster.

You get to see Babe Ruth play for the Red Sox. Better yet, you get to see him pitch.

Ruth threw four pitches to the game's first batter, Ray Morgan. Umpire Brick Owens called each one a ball, angering Ruth, who complained loudly after each call. According to Robert Creamer's wonderful biography, *Babe: The Legend Comes to Life*, after ball four Ruth asked Owens, "Why don't you open your goddamned eyes?" Owens retorted "Get the hell out of here, you're through," and gave him the thumb.

Ruth, responding in a very mature and professional manner, punched Owens in the head.

Ruth was ordered off the field and later suspended ten games. Meanwhile, Ernie Shore took over in relief, Morgan was thrown out trying to steal on the next pitch, and Shore wound up retiring the next 26 batters in order for the only perfect game ever thrown in relief.

Add it all up. A game from Fenway's earliest days. Ruth pitching. Ruth getting ejected. Ruth punching an umpire. And then a perfect game.

If something happened like that today, SportsCenter might actually explode.

DO THE CELTICS HAVE TOO MANY RETIRED NUMBERS?

14 The Celtics have retired more uniform numbers—22—than any team in the history of American sports. This figure includes one number—18—that was more or less retired twice, as it was worn first by Jim Loscutoff and, later, by Dave Cowens. No. 1 was retired in honor of team founder Walter A. Brown, and No. 2 went to the top of the Boston Garden rafters in homage to Red Auerbach, the greatest coach and general manager the National Basketball Association has ever produced.

Too many retired numbers? Look at it from this perspective: The Celtics have won 16 NBA championships, including a run of eight straight titles from 1958-59 to 1965-66. Not even the Yankees ever accomplished that.

It's hard to argue, then, that the Celtics have overdone it. But we'll make the case anyway, and for one simple reason: They *have* overdone it.

To be sure, the Celtics can assemble a fantasy team of certifiable basketball legends, which is why nobody could possibly squabble over the decision to retire the uniform numbers of Bill Russell (6), Larry Bird (33), Bob Cousy (14), John Havlicek (17), Robert Parish (00), and Kevin McHale (32).

Even if you move into a second tier of retirees, it makes sense that Hall of Famers Tom Heinsohn (15) and Sam Jones (24) have their numbers retired.

But somewhere along the way, the Celtics began giving out retired uniform numbers the way mayors hand out keys to the city.

Did Jim Loscutoff really deserve to have his number retired? He did play on seven championship teams, but he did so with the likes of Cousy, Russell, Heinsohn, and Sam Jones. He is not in the Basketball Hall of Fame.

Don Nelson, too, was a solid NBA player who averaged 11.4 points per game in his 11 seasons with the Celtics and has gone on to enjoy a splendid coaching career. But should the Celtics have retired his No. 19?

The Red Sox claim they are stingy about retiring numbers because they want to be careful about which players deserve equal billing with such legends as Ted Williams, Bobby Doerr, and Carl Yastrzemski. The Celtics, though, seem to have gone in the opposite direction: Hang around with the team long enough, play on a title team or two or three, and you'll get your number placed alongside Bill Russell's.

The height of this lunacy occurred when the Celtics retired No. 35 in memory of the late Reggie Lewis. A Celtic for six seasons, this after a stellar career at Boston's Northeastern University, Lewis collapsed during a playoff game in 1993 and died suddenly later that summer while playing pickup ball at a local college.

As we have seen, a case can be made for teams retiring the numbers of players who died before their time. But given the suspicious circumstances of Lewis' death, and longstanding accusations about his drug use, the Celtics were premature in their decision to retire No. 35.

If the Celtics truly want to honor Reggie Lewis, they should raise a question mark to the rafters.

WHAT IS THE ALL-TIME RED SOX ALL-STAR TEAM?

Each summer, Boston fans stuff the All-Star ballot box for their Sox with such zeal it's as if they were working under the express orders of James Michael Curley. But whose names would you check off if the ballot included all the players who ever wore a Red Sox uniform?

Here's our All-Time Red Sox team.

C-Carlton Fisk (1969, 71-80). Because he was a New England kid who grew up to wear the Red Sox cap on his Hall of Fame plaque. Because he was a seven-time All-Star and the gritty leader for the Sox in so many of their fights with the Yankees. Because when he hit the most famous home run in Red Sox history, we danced around the bases with him.

1B-Mo Vaughn (1991-98). Because he played one more season in Boston than Jimmie Foxx (a strong runner-up). Because of his MVP season in 1995. Because few people have worn Jackie Robinson's number so proudly or so well. "Mo proved that a black player could make it (in Boston)," Howard Bryant says.

2B-Bobby Doerr (1937-51). Because he came up with Ted from San Diego, was a perennial All-Star alongside him, and eventually joined his teammate in Cooperstown as well.

SS-Nomar Garciaparra (1996-04). Because in addition to adjusting his batting gloves 52,356 times, he batted .300 six times for the Red Sox, represented them in five All-Star games, won two batting titles, scored 100 runs six times, drove in 100 runs four times, and averaged nearly 25 home runs. And mostly because Nomah was wicked awesome.

3B-Wade Boggs (1982-92). Because he batted .300 ten times (and better than .350 five times) for the Red Sox and won five batting titles. Because he wore Red Sox colors in eight All-Star games. Because the best pure hitter of his era turned himself into an excellent fielder.

LF-Ted Williams (1939-60). Because of .406. And the Triple Crown. And the six batting titles. And the All-Star home run. And the final home run. And all the other home runs. Because even at a position with Yaz and Rice and Manny, he still is the obvious choice. Because when people saw him walking down the street, they said "There's the greatest hitter who ever lived."

CF-Tris Speaker (1907-15). Because he batted .300 seven times for Boston (including .383 in the first year at Fenway). Because there may have never been a better glove in center field. Because he led the Red Sox to two World Series championships.

RF-Dwight Evans (1972-90). Because he was a great fielder who almost hit as many home runs for Boston (379) as Rice. Because he got even better as he aged. Because he played two decades for the Red Sox and was always as dependable as the lobster at Legal Seafoods.

DH-David Ortiz (2003-present). Because of Game 4 of the 2004 ALCS. Because of Game 5 of the 2004 ALCS. Because of all those late-inning home runs and RBIs. Because as big as he seems in the batters box, his presence looms even larger in the clubhouse.

SP-Roger Clemens (1984-96). Because of that April night in 1986 when he struck out 20 batters. And that September night in 1996 when he did it again. Because of

45

all those strikeouts, all those fastballs, and all those wins. Because he should still be pitching for the Sox.

RP-Dick Radatz (1962-66). Because he not only averaged 25 saves for four seasons, he also averaged 12 wins and 135 innings. Because no one wanted to face the Monster with the game on the line.

SHOULD CELTICS BROADCASTER JOHNNY MOST BE IN THE BASKETBALL HALL OF FAME?

16 The Basketball Hall of Fame no doubt thought it was doing the right thing when, in 1993, it bestowed its Curt Gowdy Media Award to the late Johnny Most, the radio voice of the Celtics from 1953 to 1990. And surely Most was deserving of the award, which, states the Hall's website, ". . . was established by the Board of Trustees to single out members of the electronic and print media for outstanding contributions to basketball."

But in the view of the Basketball Hall of Fame, there are contributions . . . and then there are contributions. For while recipients of the Curt Gowdy Media Award are given their due at the Hall of Fame, they are not actual Hall of Famers—just as, in baseball, media members who are honored with the J. G. Taylor Spink Award are not "in" the Baseball Hall of Fame.

Take a closer look at the Basketball Hall of Fame's website, though, and you'll find a separate category for actual Hall of Famers who are enshrined as "contributors." The cast includes legendary coaches, owners, and general managers who surely did their part to make this great game what it has become.

The Hall of Fame's contributors list also includes Chick Hearn, voice of the Los Angeles Lakers from 1961 to 2002. Having already earned the Gowdy Award in 1992, Hearn, who died in 2002, was posthumously elected to the Basketball Hall of Fame in 2003.

Nobody denies that Hearn, who once called 3,338 consecutive Lakers games, is a worthy honoree. But at the risk of turning this discussion into the broadcasting version of the great Celtics-Lakers rivalry, there's just no other way to say this: If Chick Hearn is in the Hall of Fame, then Johnny Most must be in the Hall of Fame. And not merely as a Curt Gowdy Award recipient.

We can all agree that Johnny Most lacked Chick Hearn's grace and flare. Johnny didn't so much speak into the microphone as bark at it, his voice forever gravelly, raspy, smoky. And never was there a more one-sided announcer in the history of sports broadcasting; more than merely rooting on-air for his beloved Celtics, he reduced opposing players to so many hoods, thugs, and miscreants who were, according to Johnny, hell-bent on cheating their way to victory. Now and forever, onetime Washington Bullets players Rick Mahorn and Jeff Ruland will be known by the nicknames heaved upon them by Johnny Most: McFilthy and McNasty.

And, what, there's a problem with this? We're not talking about Edward R. Murrow tackling McCarthyism; we're talking about sports. It is important to remember that the Celtics struggled both for fans and media attention in the pre-Larry Bird years, despite winning championships and being led by the likes of Bill Russell, Bob Cousy, John Havlicek and other NBA legends. It was Most who fired up the masses, who got them to talking hoops, who implored them to stop what they were doing and head on down to Causeway Street and purchase a ticket.

Even Celtics fans who were not born at the time can recite some of Johnny's greatest calls, including this simple classic from the closing seconds of the 1965 Eastern Conference finals: "Havlicek stole the ball!" It's just four words, but you must hear them to appreciate them.

One wonders if the Basketball Hall of Fame has heard those four words.

WAS FREEZING TED WILLIAMS ALL THAT CRAZY?

It was bad enough when Teddy Ballgame passed away in July 2002. But when it was revealed days later that Ted's son, John Henry, had ordered the body frozen and kept in a cryonics lab in Arizona, the story changed from sorrow to tasteless comedy.

"Freeze-dried Ted," the punch-lines went. "Ted-Sicle."

The saga grew worse when the Williams family began fighting over the body amid wild rumors that what John Henry really wanted to do was sell off Ted's DNA, and worse still when we learned that the storage procedures were such that Ted's skull had several cracks in it. The only thing that would have been more appalling is placing a Hitter.net cap on the skull.

Look, we're not here to take sides in the Williams family dispute or argue what Ted really wanted. Maybe it was his final wish to be frozen, as John Henry claimed (we kind of doubt it, given that this supposed wish was written on a stained napkin). Maybe he wanted to be cremated and have his ashes spread over the Keys, as many of his friends maintained (which we think is probably the case). With John Henry dead now as well, we'll never know for sure.

And granted, at the time it happened we were among the people describing the affair as strange, sick, and twisted. But heck, we also picked the 1987 Red Sox to win it all. Now that we've had time to get used to the idea, the concept of freezing a body doesn't seem all that goofy (and the '87 Twins look like a much better bet).

Yes, it's pretty far-fetched to think that doctors will one day be able to unthaw Ted's body and not only bring him back to life, but bring him back to health as well. But 20 years ago, it was pretty far-fetched to think that Oprah Winfrey would write a bestselling fitness book. The point is, we don't know what medicine will be capable of in the future any more than we know whether our HMOs will cover the bills.

But the popular alternatives to freezing the body aren't particularly appealing, either. One, you can seal the dearly departed inside a $3,000 coffin, then bury the coffin six feet deep in the ground. The coffin will rot; worms and other insects will crawl inside and feed on the decomposing body until there is nothing remaining but bones and eventually dust. Sound unpleasant? Well, then you can always pay someone a couple thousand dollars to place the body in an incinerator and burn it in hellfire until there is nothing left but ash. Then you can place the ash in an urn and set it on the mantle next to some faded prom photos and dusty Little League trophies.

Yeah, compared to those reverent treatments, freezing the body is really out there, isn't it?

We're not saying we'd choose a cryonics lab as a final resting spot for ourselves either, but it's more practical than mummification and far less creepy than sticking Ted in a rocking chair up in the attic with Norman Bates' mother.

Again, we're not arguing over what Ted really wanted. The fact is, the only proper sendoff for Ted would have been placing a Louisville Slugger in his arms and then pushing him out to sea on an ice floe. But short of that, freezing his body in a lab is no more ghoulish than leaving it to rot under ground or burning it to a crisp.

The only real downside is if doctors one day do bring him back to life and the Yankees sign him to a five-year, $6 billion contract.

BOSTON'S GREATEST HOCKEY MYTH

 From Casey's Bar in Somerville, Massachusetts, to Doc's Tavern in Biddeford, Maine, old-time New England sports fans will quaff a 'Gansett as they tell the youngin's about the night Johnny Most, legendary Celtics play-by-play announcer, stepped behind the mike to try his hand at hockey.

The Bruins, so goes the story, needed a play-by-play pinch-hitter, whereupon Most, with no Celtics action that night, volunteered to make a temporary switch from the famous Boston Garden parquet to the ice down below.

There came a point in the game—some say the Bruins were on the offensive, others say it was their opponents—when a player took a blistering slap shot that eluded the grasp of the goaltender.

And this is where Johnny Most enters the picture.

"It hit the fuckin' post!" Most allegedly proclaimed—an unfortunate utterance that has been passed down through the generations, a sort of broadcasting gold watch handed over from father to son to grandson.

Great story. Too bad it never happened.

"It's an urban legend," said Glenn Ordway, who did Celtics broadcasts with Most for seven years in the 80s.

"Just a myth, nothing more," said Jamie Most, Johnny's son. "I think a lot of people would like it to be true, but it never happened."

Ordway remembers one night at Hartford, after the Celtics had played a game at the Civic Center, when a group of fans approached the two announcers while they were grabbing a bite to eat. One of the fans, trying to be friendly, asked Most if he remembered his famous hockey F-bomb.

"You could see Johnny tighten up and cringe," said Ordway. "Johnny was the first to admit that he used a lot of salty language, but in all the time I worked with him he never said anything like that. But I did ask him about it, and he said it probably evolved over time after he actually did do a Bruins game."

In Most's telling of the story to Ordway, both the Bruins and Celtics were playing on the west coast at the same time, in the 60s, and, to save on costs, Most was detailed to work a Bruins game. But the offensive comment was never uttered.

"Johnny always thought he might have made a comment to someone after the game, and that someone repeated it to someone else, and, next thing you know, people are saying he said it on the air," Ordway said. "But you'll never meet anyone who will tell you they actually heard it. They always say they heard it from someone else."

The closest Most ever came to saying anything truly offensive on the air? Ordway believes it may have been during a postgame show when Tom Carelli, who was producing the segment, let loose with a good-natured quip believing Most could not hear him.

Said Most, on air: "Hey, Tom, you're pretty good at math. See if you can figure out what you get if you add 2Q and 2Q."

WHAT WAS THE BIGGEST HOME RUN IN BOSTON HISTORY?

19 Choosing the biggest home run in Red Sox history is a little like determining Springsteen's best song, the sexiest Victoria's Secret model, or Boston's best Irish bar. Beginning with Babe Ruth's first career home run in 1915, there's been a lot of competition. Still, we've narrowed it down to these eight.

8. TONY C COMES BACK, APRIL 8, 1969.

After missing the final two months of the 1967 season and all of 1968 with vision problems from his beaning, Tony Conigliaro returned to the Boston lineup and hit a 10th-inning home run off Pete Richert in a 5-4 Red Sox win.

7. TED'S PENNANT CLINCHER, 1946.

Ted not only clinched the pennant with a home run in a 1-0 victory; it was an inside-the-parker, the only one of his career.

6. BABE RUTH'S LAST HOME RUN, MAY 25, 1935.

Considering he probably weighed more than Seabiscuit by then, you can't really say the Babe was a shadow of his former self when he returned to Boston with the Braves in 1935.

But he clearly wasn't the transcendent player he once had been. Ruth hit just six home runs for the Braves and batted below the Mendoza Line. But he had one Ruthian moment when he hit the final three home runs of his career—all in one game—and the last of them was as impressive as any he ever hit. Ruth drove a pitch from Guy Bush over the grandstand and out of Pittsburgh's Forbes Field, the first player to do so. It would have been one of the all-time great finishes, but he made the crucial mistake of playing a couple more games and striking out in his final at-bat.

5. TED WILLIAMS, 1941 ALL-STAR GAME.

We've all seen the film clip of Ted taking that smooth, seemingly effortless swing and then leaping up and down as he rounds the bases like a little kid whose Ritalin supply just ran out. The moment is as much a baseball signature as Rawlings.

4. TED'S FINAL AT-BAT, 1960.

Williams is one of the only players in major league history—and the only Hall of Famer—who ended his career with a home run. On a cold, drizzly day Ted stepped to the plate for one final time and sent a 1-1 pitch over the fence for the 521st and last home run of his career. And he treated it the way he treated most of them: routine, just part of the job, ma'am. He circled the bases quickly, crossed home plate, and disappeared into the dugout. Despite the cries of begging fans, he did not step out for a curtain call. As a young John Updike wrote in his splendid account of the game, "Gods don't answer letters."

3. DAVE HENDERSON, GAME 5, 1986 ALCS.

The home run turned certain defeat into a stunning lead that helped rally the Red Sox to the World Series. Trailing 5-2 in the game, and 3-1 in the series, the Red Sox scored two runs on Don Baylor's home run but were one strike away from winter when Angels reliever Donnie Moore faced Henderson, acquired from the Mariners at midseason. "He's a long way from Seattle," Al Michaels said just before Hendu launched his name into permanent Boston lore.

2. DAVID ORTIZ, GAME 4, 2004 ALCS.

When Mariano Rivera left the bullpen to pitch the ninth inning that night, we saw a father whisk his son out of Fenway Park to beat the traffic and avoid the pain. The kid asked whether the Sox had any chance to come back against Rivera and the father told him, "No. He's the best."

Such fatalism was the defining trait of Red Sox fans until the team overcame decades of heartbreak by mounting an unlikely comeback against Rivera to send the game into extra innings. And Big Papi capped that wonderful night five hours after it began by slamming the first pitch thrown to him into the stands for a two-run, walkoff homer in the

12th inning that sent the Red Sox spilling out of the dugout like foam from a popped champagne bottle. The Yankees, meanwhile, staggered off the field, wondering "What the hell just happened?"

What had just happened was that the Boston-New York rivalry had dramatically changed course. This time, the Titanic avoided the iceberg. The Red Sox trailed only one more time that October, and the franchise's fortunes were changed forever.

1. CARLTON FISK, GAME 6, 1975 WORLD SERIES.

Years after he hit it, Carlton Fisk maintained that he still hadn't watched a replay of the home run, purposely avoiding any highlights because he didn't want to have his memory of the moment altered by anything else.

We're not sure whether to believe him. Avoiding that famous videotape of Fisk waving the ball fair is akin to not seeing some epsiode of "Law and Order" while flipping through the channels. It was even used as a key scene in an Oscar-winning movie. And that essentially is why we give the nod to Fisk over Ortiz. Yeah, the Red Sox lost Game 7 the night after Fisk's homer and yeah, the Sox went on to win it all after Big Papi's shot. But while Ortiz's home run deeply touched Red Sox fans, Fisk's homer was watched by millions more people and felt across the entire country. Ortiz's home run was a milestone in Boston history—Fisk's was a milestone in baseball history.

57

WHAT WAS THE MOST OVERHYPED MOMENT IN BOSTON SPORTS HISTORY?

It was not so much a press conference as a coronation. It was carried live by all the Boston television stations, but, given all the pomp and circumstance, given the pageantry, the BBC would have been just as appropriate.

The date: May 8, 1997. The location: The new Boston Garden, at the time known as the FleetCenter. The man of the hour, of the decade, of the century: Rick Pitino.

The onetime University of Massachusetts basketball player—and, later, head coach at Boston University—was returning to the commonwealth to accept a position with the Boston Celtics. Not only was he to be the new head coach of the once-great Celtics, but he was also to assume the title of club presidency—a sort of organizational knighthood that had once belonged to Arnold "Red" Auerbach, the greatest coach in basketball history, and, arguably, in sports history.

Not only did King Richard, er, Pitino, steal Red's title; he also stole his accomplishments. The press conference was held at half court on the FleetCenter parquet, and the backdrop was provided by the Celtics' 16 NBA championship banners, which had been lowered from the rafters especially for the occasion. The audience was festooned with such former Celtics greats as M. L. Carr (the outgoing coach) and John Havlicek.

As for Red, he was given a new title: vice-chairman of the board. And just to show there were no hard feelings, Pitino allowed a photograph of a smiling, contented, cigar-puffing Auerbach to grace the cover of the Celtics' 1997-98 media guide . . . above and to the left of a photograph of Pitino.

The event brought new attention to the Celtics. There was a surge in ticket sales. And most people agreed that Pitino, who had led the University of Kentucky to three Final Four appearances in five years (including a national championship in 1996) would perform similar heroics with the Celtics. The glory days were back.

But the Celtics, coming off a 15-67 season, did not get a good bounce from the Ping-Pong ball come draft time, being unable to land the much-coveted Tim Duncan of Wake Forest, who was gobbled up by the San Antonio Spurs.

Whatever Pitino's skills as a college basketball coach, they did not translate in the NBA. He made a dizzying array of trades, none of which vaulted the Celtics back into play-off contention. He lasted three-plus seasons, skipping town 34 games into the 2000-01 season with the Celtics limping along at 12-22.

Pitino's record as head coach (and president) of the Celtics: 102-146, a .411 winning percentage.

Playoff appearances: zero.

Jim O'Brien replaced Pitino as coach. Red Auerbach, a member of the NBA since its formation in 1946, and who joined the Celtics in 1950, was later reinstated as club president.

WHICH GM WAS MOST RESPONSIBLE FOR THE RED SOX 2004 WORLD CHAMPIONSHIP?

21 When Theo Epstein temporarily left the Red Sox during the 2005-06 offseason, Boston fans reacted as if they had just learned that Jimmy Fallon was going to film a sequel to *Fever Pitch*. There was so much hysteria over his departure that Epstein literally had to sneak out of Fenway in a gorilla suit—surely the most outlandish garb seen at the ballpark that wasn't worn by Kevin Millar. And given that Epstein was the general manager when the Red Sox ended their world-championship drought, the anguish was understandable.

But which general manager really was most responsible for the 2004 championship? The man who was there when it was won or the man who was in charge when much of the team was built? Let's look at the records.

Theo took over in the winter of 2002-03 as the Macaulay Culkin of general managers, surrounded by questions and punchlines about his inexperience and youth (our favorite—that Michael Jackson had dangled him from the balcony of his hotel). But he quickly went from Macaulay Culkin to Branch Rickey. One of his first moves was signing David Ortiz, which, considering the price ($1.25 million) and the payoff, ranks among the greatest deals in major league history outside of 10-cent beer night. He signed Bill Mueller at a bargain rate; the third baseman became a batting champ. He somehow finagled Millar into a Red Sox uniform even though the first baseman already had signed with a Japanese team. He made the risky move of doing something the Red Sox never did—trade a team icon for defense—by dealing shortstop Nomar Garciaparra for Orlando Cabrera and Doug Mientkiewicz in a four-team deal more complicated than the plot to *The Matrix: Reloaded*. He also picked up Dave Roberts in time for the most important stolen base in team history.

And, of course, he also visited Curt and Shonda Schilling for a rather important Thanksgiving dinner.

That's pretty impressive, especially for someone who had just received his learner's permit.

Now, let's look at his predecessor, Dan Duquette. Mr. Popularity is best known for saying that Roger Clemens was "in the twilight of his career" and letting him leave as a free agent. This was like NBC canceling *Star Trek* because the series had outlasted its popularity and didn't have anywhere to go as a franchise. Then again, Theo let Pedro Martinez go and agreed to a trade for Alex (Mr. October) Rodriguez before the union vetoed the deal, so no one is infallible.

The rest of Duquette's record is much better. While he let Clemens go, he later traded for Pedro to replace him. He also traded for Jason Varitek and Derek Lowe and signed Tim Wakefield, Manny Ramirez, and Johnny Damon. If you're scoring at home, that means Duquette was responsible for the pitcher who won the clinching game of the 2004 ALCS and World Series (Lowe), the winner of Game 3 of the World Series (Pedro), the MVP of the World Series (Ramirez), the heart and soul of the championship team (Varitek), and Johnny "Jesus" Damon.

That's damned impressive.

Which general manager was more responsible for the Red Sox world championship? While the Red Sox wouldn't have won without the work of both, Duquette played an ever-so-slightly bigger role, if only because he had been in charge longer. Duquette wasn't popular, and he spent money like a congressman in an election year, but praising only St. Theo is like tipping the guys who installed the plasma TV and ignoring the guy who drove the delivery truck. Remember, had Roberts not stolen second base, or had the Yankees not repeatedly left the bases loaded in Game 4, the Sox would have lost the ALCS, there would have been no world championship, the team would have been dismantled and Theo would still be hearing jokes about his age.

Phil Esposito is the most prolific scorer in the history of the Bruins, a magician of the slot who knew what to do with the puck after it had been delivered to him by his two burly linemates, Wayne Cashman and Ken Hodge.

Obtained in 1967 in a trade of epic one-sidedness—he came to Boston from the Chicago Blackhawks with Hodge and Fred Stanfield for Pit Martin, Jack Norris, and Gilles Marotte—Esposito would become the NHL's first 100-point scorer, with 49 goals and 77 assists for 126 points during the 1968-69 season. And then there was Esposito's own special Spirit of 76: During the 1970-71 season, he amassed the staggering total of 76 goals and 76 assists for 152 points.

But despite all the goals, and helping to lead the Bruins to two Stanley Cups, business was, as always, business. The

B's sent Esposito to the New York Rangers in the 1975 deal that brought Jean Ratelle and Brad Park to Boston, and, four years later, they bestowed Espo's No. 7 upon a flashy young defenseman named Raymond Bourque.

Everybody was confident Bourque was on his way to becoming one of the NHL's next great players, and the kid did not disappoint. But the crime here is that the Bruins so cavalierly handed out the uniform number of a player who had performed brilliantly for the team for nearly a decade.

After Esposito's playing career ended in 1981, the Bruins attempted to mend fences by bringing their onetime scoring sensation back to the old Boston Garden for a pregame ceremony. The plan was that Espo's No. 7 would be raised to the Garden rafters, but that Bourque would continue to wear the number for the remainder of his career. (There is historical precedence for this. The Yankees gave No. 8 to Yogi Berra after veteran catcher Bill Dickey's career ended. In 1972, the team retired No. 8 in honor of both players.)

The ceremony honoring Phil Esposito took place on December 3, 1987, and, though it was expected to be an emotional affair, few anticpated the never-to-be-forgotten drama that was to unfold.

As Esposito stood on the ice in the company of former teammates and various other luminaries, Bourque, then in his 10th season with the Bruins and already a Hall of Fame lock, skated out to the spot where the ceremony was taking place. Looking Esposito square in the eye, and smiling,

Bourque then liberated himself from his sweater, with his name and No. 7 on the back, and handed the garment to this blast from the Bruins' past.

The true magnitude of the gesture was made clear when fans could see that Bourque had been wearing another sweater underneath his No. 7 sweater. And the new sweater revealed a new number for Bourque: No. 77. He would wear No. 77 for the remainder of his career, which would include, at the end, two partial seasons with the Colorado Avalanche, for whom he helped win a Stanley Cup.

Raymond Bourque had literally given Phil Esposito the shirt off his back. And the best part of it all was that the gesture did not jump out of the pages of some marketing guru's notebook. Bourque alone devised the surprise, a young star paying homage to an old legend, with 15,000 or so fans invited to witness.

DOES DOMINIC DIMAGGIO BELONG IN THE HALL OF FAME?

"Who's better than his brother Joe?
   Dom-i-nic DiMaggio" — popular refrain in Boston during late 40s and early 50s
   Talk about wishful thinking.

Joe might have been an aloof tightwad, but he was so undeniably one of the greatest players in baseball history that he received Hall of Fame votes before he was eligible. His brother, Dom, meanwhile, was a very good, extremely dependable player and a tremendous fielder. But does that make him better than his brother? Hardly. After all, just because Randy Quaid was in one of highest-grossing films ever produced, *Independence Day*, doesn't mean he's more of a box office draw than his brother, Dennis.

More importantly, though, should Dommie have a plaque in Cooperstown alongside Joe's? You can make a halfway decent case for that argument, and a number of people have. Ted Williams lobbied for years to get his good friend into the Hall of Fame through the Veterans Committee. A website was dedicated to the same goal.

Now, we hate to disagree with Ted on anything related to baseball, but he was letting his friendship get in the way of the facts here. Look at the record.

In Dom's favor, he played in seven All-Star games, received MVP votes six seasons, and finished in the top 10 in batting three times. He scored more than 100 runs six times and twice had an on-base percentage above .400. As good a center fielder as Joe was, Dom might have been even better. He was a leader on some of the best teams in Red Sox history.

No denying it. He was a very good player. On the other hand, with only ten seasons (not counting his final year,

1953, when he batted three times) Dom just meets the bare minimum requirement for consideration. He batted .300 only four times, including his rookie year in 1940 when he had only 418 at-bats. He had little power, averaging fewer than nine home runs a season. His lifetime average was under .300 (though just under at .298).

While it's not Dom's fault that he lost three full seasons while serving his country in World War II, you can't give him credit for those missing seasons any more than you can give Trot Nixon credit for all the games he missed on the disabled list. If the Hall of Fame enshrined all the "If only" candidates, it would need to move to someplace bigger, like the Pentagon or Shaquille O'Neal's house.

Look, from all accounts, Dom DiMaggio is an intelligent and fine man and he was a damn fine ballplayer. But he's not a Hall of Famer. If you really want to make a case for a great fielder who was snubbed by the Hall voters, we nominate Dwight Evans. Dewey was as good a fielder (eight Gold Gloves) as Dom and a far more productive batter with 385 home runs (and that was back when home runs meant something), almost 1,400 runs, and more than 1,400 RBIs.

Dewey isn't in the Hall of Fame, either, and there's no shame in that. Being remembered as merely one of the great players in Red Sox history isn't such a bad legacy.

WHAT WAS THE MOST EMBARRASSING ON-ICE MOMENT IN BRUINS HISTORY?

24 If May 10, 1970 is the proudest day in Bruins history, what with Bobby Orr's famous (but not greatest) goal lifting the B's to their first Stanley Cup championship in 29 years, then May 10, 1979—exactly nine years later—goes into the books as the most embarrassing day in Bruins history.

The easiest way to make the case is with six simple words: Too many men on the ice. To say those six words to a Bruins fan is akin to walking up to Joe Namath and saying, "Hey, Joe, tell us about that Suzy Kolber interview again."

The 1978-79 Bruins posted a 43-23-14 record, their 100 points earning them first place in the Adams Division. Bobby Orr and Phil Esposito were gone, but the Bruins had a balanced scoring attack led by Rick Middleton and Peter McNab, a talented tough guy in Terry O'Reilly, the veteran leadership of Jean Ratelle and Brad Park, and a solid goaltending tandem in oldie-but-goodie Gerry Cheevers and young Gilles Gilbert.

The Bruins, it was felt, were good enough to win it all. They took out the Pittsburgh Penguins in the first round of the playoffs, and were then matched up with the Montreal Canadiens in the second round, the two teams deadlocked after six games.

Game 7 was played on May 10, 1979 at the Forum, and the Bruins, clinging to a 4-3 lead, were two minutes and 34 seconds away from ridding themselves of the Canadiens.

But then something went terribly wrong on the Bruins bench. To this day nobody is precisely sure how it happened, but the Bruins wound up with too many men on the ice. This did not go unnoticed by referee John D'Amico.

Blessed with a power play, the Canadiens tied the game with 24 seconds remaining in regulation when Guy Lafleur fired a slap shot past Gilbert, who appeared to be screened. The Canadiens then won the game, and the series, at 9:33 of overtime on a goal by Yvon Lambert.

So . . . too many men on the ice. Good call? Bad call? It depends on whether you read the papers the morning after the game, or a day later.

Bruins general manager Harry Sinden, with predictable outrage, talked about the "invisible" extra man D'Amico had seen. Bruins coach Don Cherry said that the officiating "overshadowed a magnificent effort." Bruins player Bob Miller told reporters, "There are 20 guys across the way who know they're pretty lucky right now," referring, of course, to the Canadiens.

69

A day later, the Bruins came to the conclusion that D'Amico's call was correct.

"There was no problem about it," Cherry told the *Boston Herald American*. "We deserved the penalty, and there is only one guy to blame—me. I'm the captain of the ship. Hell, I grabbed two of them or there would have been eight of them on the ice."

There is no Bill Buckner-esque culprit here. The Bruins simply got mixed up at a rather unfortunate juncture in the game. Even Sinden changed his tune, explaining that when the penalty was called he was under the stands watching the game on television, but that his assistant, former Bruins coach Tom Johnson, later told him it was "a flagrant violation."

The Canadiens went on to whip the New York Rangers in five games to win the Stanley Cup.

The Bruins went back to the blackboard . . . something they've been doing every year since.

WHAT WAS THE MOST EMBARRASSING OFF-ICE MOMENT IN BRUINS HISTORY?

25 If the life of the Boston Bruins fan were a television game show, the events of June 9, 2001 would have been referred to as a "consolation prize." Or, a "lovely parting gift." For it was on that night that the Colorado Avalanche captured their second Stanley Cup, emerging with a 3-1 victory over the New Jersey Devils.

It was big news out in Denver, and, by extension, big news for those fans of the Boston Bruins who were so inclined as to press their noses up against the glass to watch Aves fans celebrate their team's championship.

This was a Bruins fan's consolation prize, the lovely parting gift. For in latching on to a piece of the Aves' Stanley Cup celebration, what B's fans were really doing was paying homage to one of the greatest Bruins of all time, Raymond Bourque, who was closing out his career in Colorado after 21 stellar seasons in Boston. The Hall of Fame-bound defenseman was finally going to get his name engraved on the world's most famous sports trophy, and

Bruins fans, having come to terms with the cold, hard reality that the man was never going to win a championship in Boston, could not have been happier for Bourque.

It was in the spring of 2000 that the going-nowhere Bruins put Bourque in a position to win a Stanley Cup by sending him to the Avalanche in exchange for Brian Rolston, Martin Grenier, Samuel Pahlsson, and a first-round draft pick. The Aves didn't get the job done in 2000, but the following year, inspired by their new leader, they did win a Stanley Cup.

One of the really cool, quirky traditions of the Stanley Cup is that those who win it get to possess it. Each player, each coach, earns the right to "own" the Cup for a while, to show it off to the friends and neighbors. But for Bourque, showing off the Cup involved a whole lot more than a backyard barbeque and a truckload of beer.

It involved a citywide celebration.

On June 12, 2001, just three days after the Avalanche eliminated the Devils, Raymond Bourque returned to Boston. And he brought a friend: the Stanley Cup. The City of Boston embraced the moment by staging a celebration at Government Center, with between 15,000 and 20,000 fans turning out to see Bourque hoist the Cup over his head.

Now, understand that Government Center and the Stanley Cup are old friends. Built upon the ruins of the infamous, bawdy Scollay Square, Government Center opened in the late 60s, just in time to host two Stanley Cup championship celebrations when the B's won the Cup in 1970 and 1972.

This was different, of course. For here were thousands of Bruins fans—OK, Raymond Bourque fans—turning out essentially to celebrate another city's Stanley Cup celebration. It had to be a long, embarrassing day for the management of the Bruins, locked down at their offices on nearby Causeway Street while Bourque hoisted his Stanley Cup into the air.

The symbolism was shocking: The Bruins once owned this town, could do no wrong. Now things had gotten so bad that their fans were reduced to celebrating another team's Stanley Cup season.

WHO WAS THE BEST PITCHER IN RED SOX HISTORY?

26 Thanks in part to Fenway Park, the Red Sox will always be known for their hitters. But they've also enjoyed some of the finest pitchers in major league history, including the man for whom pitching's highest honor is named.

Yeah, Roger Clemens won seven Cy Young awards but consider this: Clemens won a career-high 24 games in 1986, whereas Young *averaged* 24 wins a season for eight years with the Red Sox. He had back-to-back 30-win seasons. He averaged 41 starts a season. He pitched the Sox to their first World Series championship. And he won 511 games in his career, almost 200 more than Clemens.

But let's face it: Young pitched old mushy baseballs stained by tobacco juice to teams of malnourished white dwarves with bad teeth and worse breath that swung four-pound piano table legs for bats. The competition Young faced was vastly inferior compared to today's 6-4, 250-pound monsters of every color and nationality who are breast-fed creatine as babies then raised on a 6,000-calorie-a-day diet of steroid-injected beef and Jethroe-sized bowls of Wheaties.

Similarly, Smoky Joe Wood and Babe Ruth also were pitching with a dead ball back when a 3.73 ERA got you a train ticket to the minors instead of a four-year, $60 million contract. While Lefty Grove won 300 games, he was well past his prime before reaching Boston for his final seven seasons and 105 victories. Grove, Luis Tiant, and Curt Schilling all made their marks elsewhere.

Really, this debate comes down to Clemens and the man who essentially replaced him, Pedro Martinez.

Clemens won 192 games for the Red Sox, including three 20-win seasons and three Cy Young awards. He was 24-4 in 1986, was named the MVP, won the All-Star Game and took a no-hitter into the fifth inning of Game 6 of the World Series before . . . well, no need to go into that here. He twice struck out 20 batters in a game. But in his last four seasons in Boston he reached his standard 200-inning mark just once and was basically a .500 pitcher (40-39). Dan Duquette might have been dead wrong but he wasn't a complete moron when he decided Clemens was in the twilight of his career and let him go after the 1996 season.

What made that decision somewhat less painful was the addition of Martinez two years later. As dominant as Clemens had been in the late 80s and early 90s, Pedro was every bit as good during his seven years with the Red Sox, winning an astounding 76 percent of his decisions (Clemens won 63 percent of his Boston starts). He twice won 20 games, as well as the Cy Young award, and would have won the 1999 MVP as well had two writers not left his name entirely off the ballot. Pound for pound, no one may have ever been better than Pedro that season when he went 23-4 with a 2.07 ERA and 313 strikeouts, not including whiffing the first five batters in the All-Star Game and 23 batters in the postseason.

So, who was better while in a Red Sox uniform, the Rocket or Pedro? It's a tough call, like choosing between Sam Adams Boston Lager and Sam Adams Pale Ale.

What it essentially comes down to is this: The two each had seven spectacular seasons when they were the best or nearly the best pitcher in the league. So it depends on whether you give Clemens bonus credit for his six additional seasons with the Sox or penalize him for having additional mediocre seasons.

We go with Clemens, because though he was just above .500 those seasons, the crucial fact is he was pitching, he was helping the Sox win, and he was much better than the alternative. He may not have been up to his usual standards or as dominant as Pedro, but he was a damn sight better than Vaughn Eshelman, Jeff Suppan, or Nate Minchey.

WHAT WAS THE WORST TIME IN HISTORY TO BE A BOSTON SPORTS FAN?

27 During the Red Sox' "Impossible Dream" season of 1967, the *Boston Globe* nicely summed up the pulse of the region with this never-to-be-forgotten headline: "Pennant Fever Grips Hub."

In the last days of the 20th century and continuing right on into the dawning of the 21st century, a better headline might have been: "Playoff Funk Grips Hub."

Not only were Boston's professional sports franchises struggling during this period, they had all but disappeared from the map. It was a millennium malaise: During the last year of the 20th century (2000) and the first year of the 21st century (2001) not a single postseason game was played by the Red Sox, Patriots, Bruins, or Celtics.

The exact duration of the drought was two years, three months, and one day. And while nobody knew it at the time, it all began on the night of October 18, 1999, when the Red Sox dropped a 6-1 decision to the New York Yankees and were eliminated from the American League Championship Series in five games.

It would not be until January 19, 2002, that another post-season game would be played by a Boston sports team. And it would be the Patriots who would end the malaise, doing so in historic fashion with their 16-13 overtime victory against the Oakland Raiders in the "Snow Game" at Foxboro Stadium.

What a long wait it had been for Boston sports fans. This is a sports market that boasts several Celtics dynasties, dating all the way back to 1957. This is a town that, in the early 70s, embraced Bobby Orr and the Big, Bad Bruins. As for the Red Sox, there was always this: Though it seemed like they'd never win a World Series, they went into each new season with the expectation that they'd be competing for a postseason run.

But there were no visits to the postseason in 2000, or in 2001. Not for the Red Sox, not for anybody. Passion remained high, if game attendance and sports talk-radio ratings count for anything, but the reward for all the passion was game after game after game of subpar performance.

All four teams were trying to fix things on the fly. Beginning with the 2000 season, Bill Belichick replaced

Pete Carroll as head coach of the Patriots. Late in the 2001 season, the Red Sox fired manager Jimy Williams and replaced him with Joe Kerrigan, who would himself get fired when new owners took over the Red Sox during spring training in 2002. Mike Keenan, the master of the quick fix, replaced Pat Burns as coach of the Bruins in October 2000. He fixed nothing. And it was also during this period, midway through the 2001-02 season, that Rick Pitino stepped down as coach of the Celtics.

Boston had become . . . Loserville.

The word, as it applies to the Boston sports community, was first used by *Boston Herald* columnist Gerry Callahan.

And unlike most of the athletes he was covering at the time, Callahan was on target with his shot.

WHICH WAS THE MOST IMPORTANT SEASON IN RED SOX HISTORY?

28

No, sorry. You're wrong. While 2004 was a great season, it wasn't the most important.

Sure, finally winning the World Series made everyone feel a whole lot better (and let others die with smiles on their faces the width of the Zakim Bridge), but it's not like the team wasn't already a beloved part of the city. The Red Sox already were selling out Fenway Park, broadcast ratings already were sky high, and Boston already was established as one of the game's richest, most competitive, and best-run teams.

The 1967 season was different. Hard as it is to believe now, there was a time when the city didn't live and die by the Red Sox, when a manager's poor decision Tuesday night didn't automatically prompt calls for his dismissal all Wednesday afternoon on talk radio. For one thing, there weren't 24-hour sports stations back then. More importantly, the city was apathetic—it wasn't Red Sox Nation, more like Red Sox Unincorporated Municipality. The Sox, after all, had finished one-half game out of last place the previous season. They had played in the World Series

79

exactly once in 48 years and hadn't reached it in 21. They drew only 811,000 fans in 1966 (and just 652,000 in 1965) and there was talk of tearing down Fenway Park—which was viewed as simply old rather than classic — and replacing it with one of those cookie cutter, multipurpose stadiums that were all the rage. Moving out of Boston wasn't beyond the realm of possibility.

How bad was it? They drew 8,234 for the 1967 home opener.

Forever remembered as the "Impossible Dream," the ensuing season changed all that. From the April day when rookie Billy Rohr nearly pitched a no-hitter in his first start, all New England was infected with Red Sox Fever. They cheered Rohr's name in April, gasped in horror that awful August evening when Tony Conigliaro took a Jack Hamilton fastball to the face ("It sounded like a pumpkin smashing," Dick Williams once described it) and had their spirits lifted as high as Carl Yastrzemski's bat whenever he stepped into the box. And remember, this was before the Internet, before ESPN, and before SportsCenter. When the Sox played on the west coast, New England went to bed not knowing whether the Sox won or lost.

How did we survive? It's not only a miracle anyone got any sleep that summer, it's a wonder anyone had any cuticles left when the Sox finally won the pennant.

The Sox lost in the World Series, of course, defeated by the Cardinals and the great Bob Gibson. It didn't really matter much, though. The Sox had recaptured Boston's soul and they never let it go again. The Red Sox have been competitive almost every year since (just five losing seasons), and attendance has often been near the top of the league despite playing in the league's smallest ballpark.

"It's what lit the fuse for Red Sox baseball," Jim Lonborg says. "They'd had some good years in the 1940s but there had been a lot of mediocrity for a long time since then. That sparked it."

(And here are two great trivia questions from 1967 to pose in a bar. One, who pinch-ran for Conigliaro? If they know that it was Jose Tartabull—and they should if they're true Red Sox fans—give them this follow up: Hamilton is remembered as a headhunter but how many batters did he hit in 1967? Just one. Conigliaro. By the way, Tartabull came around to score as the pinch-runner that inning and the Red Sox won the game by one run en route to a pennant decided by one victory.)

WHAT WAS BOSTON'S GREATEST MIGHT-HAVE-BEEN POWERHOUSE?

The Boston Braves played their final home game on September 21, 1952, an 8-2 loss to the Brooklyn Dodgers at Braves Field. The season would come to a merciful end a week later at Ebbets Field, with the Braves and Dodgers playing to a 12-inning, 5-5 tie. There hadn't been much to play for that day. The Dodgers had already wrapped up the National League pennant, whereas the seventh-place Braves had wrapped up nothing more than train tickets home.

By the following spring, rumor and speculation turned into sobering reality for Braves fans: The team announced it was leaving Boston and relocating to Milwaukee. The Braves had drawn only 281,278 fans to Braves Field in '52, while Boston's American League entry, the Red Sox, despite finishing 19 games in back of the pennant-winning Yankees, had drawn 1,115,750 fans to Fenway Park.

The message was clear: Boston could only support one big-league baseball team.

Yet the question must be asked, all these years later, could that team have been the Braves?

The answer is yes.

It's difficult to imagine in this modern era of Red Sox Nation, with fans packing Fenway Park from April to October. But consider the possibility of a Braves Nation: At the time the team left town, it already had the makings of a powerhouse, with Warren Spahn and Lew Burdette on the pitching staff, a fiery young Johnny Logan at shortstop, and a future Hall of Famer named Eddie Mathews at third base. Oh, and down in the minors there was a kid named Hank Aaron, a former Negro Leaguer who had signed with the Boston Braves on June 14, 1952.

Comfortably settled in their new home at Milwaukee's County Stadium, the Braves enjoyed a great run through most of the 1950s. In 1953, their first season in Milwaukee, the Braves jumped to second place in the National League, with Spahn winning 23 games and Mathews clubbing a league-leading 47 home runs.

The Braves dipped to third place in '54, but still won 89 games. Spahn won 21 games. Aaron, on his way to becoming the greatest home run hitter in baseball history, enjoyed a respectable rookie season.

After second-place finishes in '55 and '56, the Braves captured the National League pennant in 1957 and then took out the Yankees in the World Series, with Burdette winning three games, including a seven-hit shutout in the deciding seventh game.

The 1958 season would produce another pennant for the Braves, who this time lost to the Yankees in the World Series. In '59, the Braves finished just two games behind the pennant-winning Dodgers, now enjoying themselves in Los Angeles.

In their first eight seasons away from Boston, the Braves had won two pennants, placed second five times and finished third once. And three of their stars—Aaron, Spahn, and Mathews—were headed for Cooperstown.

As for the Red Sox, they were little more than a middle-of-the-pack outfit through most of the '50s. Their home attendance actually went down in 1953, the Sox' first season as Boston's lone big-league team; from 1953 to 1956, they finished in fourth place. By 1960, Ted Williams' last season, the Sox were a seventh-place club, trailed only by the Kansas City Athletics.

Would the Braves have had the same brand of success in the 1950s had they remained in Boston? Again, the building blocks were in place. Spahn. Aaron. Mathews.

It would have been fun to watch.

WHICH SOX WORLD SERIES TEAM WAS THE BEST?

30 The 2004 Red Sox won the team's first world championship in 86 years, became the first team in major league history to rally from a 3-0 series deficit in the postseason and the only team to have a lead in every inning of the World Series, were named *Sports Illustrated's* Sportsmen of the Year, and were immortalized in *Fever Pitch* (though we won't hold that against them). They rightfully will be the most beloved team in franchise history.

But does that mean they were more talented than the World Series teams that fell short in 1946, 1967, 1975, and 1986? Short of the world's most realistic video game, we'll never know, but that doesn't stop us from making a guess.

1946: This was the team of Ted Williams, Bobby Doerr, Johnny Pesky, and Dom DiMaggio, a team that should have played in several World Series, not just one. And perhaps they would have had Boston the foresight to sign a proven leader like Jackie Robinson (see argument 7). Without a single minority on the roster, it's impossible to consider this team in the same league as the others.

Sigh. If only the Sox had been ahead of the curve on integration instead of way behind it.

1967: The "Impossible Dream" team that resurrected Boston baseball. This was Yaz's finest season and he absolutely carried the team—he won the Triple Crown, but no one else drove in as many as 83 runs. The pitching staff wasn't exceptional, boosted by Jim Lonborg in by far his best season.

Sigh. If only Tony C. hadn't been beaned. . . .

1975: Looking back at this team, the question is not how it didn't win the World Series but how it didn't win the next five as well. You had perhaps the best outfield in Red Sox history, with rookies Fred Lynn and Jim Rice, plus 23-year-old Dwight Evans—and Carl Yastrzemski returned to left when Rice broke his wrist at the end of the season. Hall of Fame catcher Carlton Fisk was behind the plate for Rick Wise, Luis Tiant, and Bill Lee. Rico Petrocelli was at third and Rich Burleson at short. This was a team so deep that Cecil Cooper was on the bench much of the time.

Sigh. If only Rice hadn't gotten hurt.

1986: Evans started the season by hitting the very first pitch into the seats and the Sox never slowed. Roger Clemens was at his best with a good rotation around him—Bruce Hurst, the volatile Oil Can Boyd, and Tom Seaver in his final season. The outfield was good but not great with Rice in his final MVP-type season and Evans near his peak but Tony Armas in decline (with Dave Henderson subbing famously in the postseason). Wade Boggs hit .357 at third and Bill Buckner drove in 102 runs at first, but the infield was mediocre up the middle with Spike Owen at short and Marty Barrett at second. Don Baylor hit 31 home runs with 94 RBIs as the DH.

Sigh. Had it not been for Calvin Schiraldi. . . .

2004: They were so good that they felt they could trade away Nomar Garciaparra. They had one can't-miss Hall of Famer in Pedro Martinez, plus two possible Hall of Famers in Manny Ramirez and Curt Schilling. A good catcher in Jason Varitek and an excellent leadoff man in Johnny Damon. Mark Bellhorn and Kevin Millar had fine years, and there was a dependable closer (Keith Foulke). But the most important player may have been the DH, Big Papi, David Ortiz. There's no doubt this was a powerful lineup with a great 1-2 pitching punch. And they were on an incredible roll in late October. But were they better than the 1975 team? Heck, the 2004 club didn't even win its division.

Yes, the Cardinals team the Red Sox swept in the World Series was a good team with an extremely potent lineup of Albert Pujols, Scott Rolen, Jim Edmonds, and Larry Walker. Their pitching staff lacked a true ace, however, after Chris Carpenter got hurt.

The 1967 and 1986 Red Sox, meanwhile, had the misfortune of playing what were probably the best teams of each decade and still took both to the limit. The 1975 Red Sox had the worse misfortune of playing perhaps the best team in history and yet they still held a lead in Game 7 as late as the sixth inning. And while most people acknowledge Cincinnati's prowess, too many forget that the Sox ended the three-year reign of the decade's other dynasty by whipping Oakland in the playoffs.

Boston's best World Series team? The 2004 Sox just barely lose out to the '75 Sox, a team so good it didn't need a *Queer Eye for the Straight Guy* makeover.

WHAT WAS THE GREATEST PUBLIC RELATIONS GIMMICK IN BOSTON SPORTS HISTORY?

31 When Billy Sullivan reported for spring training in 1947 to begin his new job as public relations director of the Boston Braves, he found a skeptical crowd of sportswriters waiting for him.

This Sullivan, he was a football guy, they all said. He had worked for Boston College football coach Frank Leahy, and then moved to South Bend, Indiana, when Leahy took over the Notre Dame program. As for that popular syndicated column for King Features that appeared under Leahy's byline, well, that was ghosted by none other than Billy Sullivan.

Meeting the Boston writers at the Braves' spring training base in Fort Lauderdale, Florida, Sullivan told the boys he had written a book, titled *All That I Know About Baseball*. He gave a copy to the writers. The pages were blank. Get it? Sullivan, in laughing at himself, had defeated the writers at their own game. From that point on, they accepted Billy Sullivan as a baseball man.

And so it was that, on Opening Day, 1947, when Billy Sullivan offered free laundry service to anyone who had attended the game, the press ate it up.

Here's what happened. Braves Field, the team's aging ballpark on Commonwealth Avenue, little more than a mile from Fenway Park, had undergone a rigorous off-season sprucing-up. This included detailing a crew of workers to apply a fresh coat of paint to every seat in the joint. Turns out the seats weren't quite dry on Opening Day, and chaos ensued. Fans complained about the paint rubbing off on their clothes.

What to do? It could have been, should have been, a public relations nightmare for the Braves. Sullivan, thinking on the fly, announced a plan by which fans could send the offended clothes out to the cleaner's, and then send the bill to the Boston Braves. They didn't even have to include a ticket stub from the game.

Sullivan, who died in 1998, always laughed when he recounted the gimmick, admitting that he had no idea if the bills he received were from legitimate Opening Day attendees. But, as the Braves were forever competing with the Red Sox for the hearts and dollars of New England baseball fans, he figured it was a small price to pay for all the publicity.

To this day, old-time Braves fans have fond memories of Billy Sullivan's Opening Day laundry stunt.

Sullivan did not accompany the Braves to Milwaukee when the team left town in 1953. Though he implemented many other gimmicks during his days with the Braves—he always insisted that his inundating of out-of-town writers with dazzling statistical packages relating to the performance of Bob Elliott helped the Braves' third baseman cop the 1947 National League MVP Award—Sullivan left the team at the end of 1952 and moved to Hollywood to try his hand in the burgeoning television industry.

On November 16, 1959, Billy Sullivan raised $25,000, including $8,300 of his own money, and became the first owner of the Boston Patriots in the newly-formed American Football League.

WHAT WAS THE WORST PUBLIC RELATIONS GIMMICK IN BOSTON SPORTS HISTORY?

32 Denis Leary is a Massachusetts-born actor/comedian whose hit television series *Rescue Me* is a brilliantly written take on what it's like to be a New York firefighter. After a 1999 warehouse fire in his hometown of Worcester claimed the lives of six firefighters—including a cousin and a childhood friend—Leary responded by establishing the Leary Firefighters Foundation. In the aftermath of the September 11 terrorist strikes, he added a wing to his original foundation, calling it New York's Bravest.

Leary also played hockey growing up, and over the years he has gathered various celebrities and retired athletes to stage benefit hockey games for his foundation. Put all this together—his local roots, his passion for hockey, his philanthropy, his star power—and it just made sense for the Boston Bruins to enlist Leary for a new advertising campaign for the 2005-06 National Hockey League season.

With the NHL trying to win back its fan base following the labor strife that had doomed the entire 2004-05 season, the Bruins' plan was to market their players as a collection of tough, blue-collar guys who were more soldiers than stars. It was an attempt to rekindle images of the days of the Big, Bad Bruins, when the likes of Wayne Cashman and Ken Hodge worked the corners and feisty little muckers like John McKenzie made life miserable for bigger, stronger opponents.

And who better to deliver this message than lifelong Bruins fan Denis Leary?

The name of the ad campaign: "It's Called Bruins."

"The Bruins are Boston," says Leary in one of the TV spots. "Not the glitz, but the grit. The Bruins are where character and teamwork matter over individual achievement. The Bruins are the drumbeat of a tribe that is Boston . . . played in the neighborhood, heard in the bars, and felt in the streets. It's about the Cup. Get to work."

The spots would have worked brilliantly, save for one problem: The team Leary was pitching, the one more interested in the grit than the glitz, turned out to be horrifically bad. It was apparent just weeks into the season that the blueprint for the 2005-06 Bruins was ill conceived, and that no Stanley Cup would be coming to Boston any time soon.

To make matters worse, Bruins general manager Mike O'Connell traded the team's best player, Joe Thornton. Late in the season, the Bruins dumped another young star, Sergei Samsanov.

Fans began to mock the ad campaign. "It's Called Bruins" turned into "It's Called Ruins," or "It's called Losing." And this beauty: "Sucking: It's Called Bruins."

By the end of the season, the Bruins had amassed just 74 points, landing them in 13th place in the 15-team Eastern Conference. Yet things got worse. O'Connell had been jettisoned as general manager, but the man purportedly brought in to replace him, Ray Shero, instead took a job with the Pittsburgh Penguins. When the Bruins finally hired Peter Chiarelli as their new general manager, their fans knew they were being introduced to the team's No. 2 choice.

In the end, the Bruins had neither grit nor glitz.

BILL RUSSELL DESERVES SOMETHING NAMED AFTER HIM

33 Now that we've established Russell is the greatest athlete in Boston history, we pose this question: Why the hell hasn't anything been named in his honor? A street, boulevard, highway, tunnel, bridge, arena, park, court, traffic circle, bus stop —something?

Ted Williams has a tunnel (and deservedly so). Tom Yawkey has a Way (not so deservedly so). Reggie Lewis has a center. Heck, Johnny Pesky at least has a pole. But there is nothing for the athlete responsible for more championships in the city than anyone else.

This is a terrible oversight. Russell meant a great deal to Boston sports, not only for his great performance on the court but for all he overcame off it as the city's first African American sports star. When he moved into a house in Reading, some residents tried to block the purchase. Bigots later broke into his home and vandalized it with racial epithets.

Did Yaz ever have to put up with this?

Fortunately, it's not too late to acknowledge all that Russell did by naming something after him. And it needs to be something meaningful, not just some seldom-used alley or side street like many cities rename for a recently retired athlete. There's nothing wrong with Mazeroski Way or Kirby Puckett Place or Edgar Martinez Drive but those streets are of so minimal use that the only people who even notice them are fans and tourists looking for a photo opportunity ("Look, that's me placing a bet underneath the Pete Rose street sign"). Someone of Russell's stature deserves more. He warrants a road or structure that looms as large on the Boston cityscape as he himself did on the Garden's parquet. He requires something that is frequently mentioned in rush hour traffic reports so that everyone is constantly reminded of him ("The Ted Williams Tunnel is backed up but there's an open lane to the hoop on the Bill Russell Expressway").

Given that Ted got a tunnel, Russell deserves the

Sumner Tunnel at a minimum. Or perhaps fans should take it upon themselves to call the new Garden the Bill Russell Garden instead of the corporate name the suits want you to call it. After all, a bank may have paid $120 million for the naming rights to the arena but did we ever receive a dime of those payments? Of course not. The only thing the bank ever sends us are $10 overdraft charges for not having enough money in our accounts to cover a check for two seats in the balcony.

Better yet, they should go even further. In a real attempt to show Celtics pride and make up for past wrongs, they should honor Russell by naming an entire town after him. And we know just the one.

How does changing the name of Reading, Massachusetts, to Bill Russell, Massachusetts, sound?

WHO WAS THE GREATEST CLUTCH PERFORMER IN BRUINS HISTORY?

The easiest, most convenient way to dispatch with this business of naming the Bruins' greatest all-time clutch performer is to put up four fingers—for No. 4, Bobby Orr—and he done with it.

Orr, after all, is arguably (inarguably, some would say) the greatest player in hockey history. In addition to being a great defenseman, and a great offensive defenseman, he was also a career-long mainstay on the Bruins' power play and penalty-killing unit.

So there. Bobby Orr. Greatest clutch performer in Bruins history.

But wait. Let's approach this discussion from a different perspective. The Bruins of the Bobby Orr-Phil Esposito era were, in addition to being a rough-and-tumble bunch, one of the most feared offensive juggernauts in hockey history. In 1969, Phil Esposito became the first player in NHL history to amass 100 points in a season. During the 1970-71 season, the Bruins had four 100-point scorers (Esposito, Orr, John Bucyk, Ken Hodge), and seven of the NHL's top 10 scorers.

But even though the Bruins should have won more than just two Stanley Cups (1970 and 1972) during this era, they might not have won any without goaltender Gerry Cheevers.

Cheevers, who was inducted in the Hockey Hall of Fame in 1985, helped give the Bruins' offense some of its oomph. Had the Big, Bad Bruins not had a capable goaltending tandem (Eddie Johnston wasn't bad, either), it's possible their offense wouldn't have been so freewheeling. Cheevers was known as a "money goaltender," and for all the reasons the term applies. He made big saves, and he came up big in big games. That may sound simplistic, but here's the backbone of the discussion: In 1970, when the Bruins won their first Stanley Cup since 1941, Cheevers was in the nets for 13 of the team's 14 playoff games, posting a 12-1 record and 2.23 goals-against average. When they won the Cup again in 1972, he was in the nets for eight of 15 games, with a 6-2 record and 2.61 GAA.

But more than all that, Cheevers was a steady, consistent presence in the nets and a phenomenal skater. Unafraid to venture out of the net, he often seemed to appear from out of nowhere on viewers' television screens as a sixth skater.

Originally the property of the Toronto Maple Leafs—he played two games for the Leafs during the 1961-62 season—Cheevers made it back to the NHL, as a Bruin, during the '65-66 season. He became a Bruins mainstay during the '67-68 season. He left the team to play for the Cleveland Crusaders in the late, great World Hockey Association after the '72 Cup campaign, but returned late in the '75-76 season.

Cheevers could just as well contribute to yet another chapter in this book: "Provider of Boston's Greatest Sports Artifact." His famous goalie mask, with its intricate stitches (symbolic of the gashes he'd have received were he not wearing the thing) is now on display in the Hockey Hall of Fame.

WHO WAS THE GREATEST CLUTCH PERFORMER IN PATRIOTS HISTORY?

What separates Adam Vinatieri from most of Boston's greatest all-time athletes—in any sport—is the anonymity of his arrival.

Bobby Orr, upon touching down in Boston, was already being trumpeted as hockey's next great superstar. Larry Bird, the day he signed his first NBA contract, was the man who would introduce Celtics fans to a new dynasty. And Carl Yastrzemski did not merely replace the great Ted Williams in left field, he was his heir.

There was no such parade of expectation and hyperbole when Vinatieri arrived. Signed by the Patriots as a rookie free agent in 1996, he had come to Foxboro by way of the Amsterdam Admirals of the World League of American Football, this after playing his college ball at humble North Dakota State.

Yet that's part of the charm that is Adam Vinatieri—that this man, in a land of Orrs and Russells, Birds and Teddy Ballgames, could emerge as the New England Patriots' representative in the pantheon of Boston's greatest clutch performers.

Any telling of the adventures of Adam Vinatieri must begin on January 19, 2002, with the Patriots' 16-13 overtime playoff victory against the Oakland Raiders. In what will forever be known as the Snow Game, Vinatieri booted one of the greatest field goals in NFL history, a 45-yarder in a blinding snowstorm, and with 32 seconds remaining in regulation, to send this classic into overtime. He then kicked a 32-yard field goal to win it. With the hulking, still-under-construction Gillette Stadium rising in the background, Vinatieri's game-winning kick had yet another distinction: It ended the last Patriots game ever to be played at Foxboro Stadium.

Fans of the Raiders had a different moniker for the game. They called it the Tuck Bowl, or some such contrivance, after an apparent fumble by quarterback Tom Brady late in the game was overturned by the officials in adherence with the league's tuck rule. But while the Pats may have caught a break (so sayeth bitter Raiders fans), Vinatieri still had to get the snow and the stars and the nostalgia out of his eyes and make the kick. And he did.

The Pats were heavy underdogs against the St. Louis Rams in Super Bowl XXXVI, but, improbably, the game was tied when Vinatieri kicked a 48-yard field goal as time expired to give the Pats a 20-17 victory and the first championship in the history of this long-suffering franchise.

There would be more. In 2003, it was Vinatieri's 46-yard field goal with 4:06 remaining in the game that lifted the

Patriots to a 17-14 playoff victory over the Tennessee Titans. In the AFC title game a week later, he tied an NFL playoff record with five consecutive field goals in the Pats' 24-14 victory over the Indianapolis Colts. And in Super Bowl XXXVIII, Vinatieri's 41-yard field goal with four seconds remaining was the difference as the Pats defeated the Carolina Panthers, 32-29.

It's easy to discount Vinatieri's accomplishments, to say that, well, he's just a kicker—or to point out that, in the grand scheme, Brady, the quarterback, was more "important" to the success of the Patriots.

But Vinatieri made the kick in the snow that night. It was at that point that the Pats' great postseason run—three Super Bowl championships in four years—got its start.

WHO WAS THE GREATEST CLUTCH PERFORMER IN RED SOX HISTORY?

What you're about to read is a true story, as well as a really neat look into inner workings of the publishing industry.

Fact: This is the last chapter that was written for this book. It was being re-worked and re-worked on the night of

July 31, 2006, with a case being made that Carl Yastrzemski is the greatest clutch performer in Red Sox history.

The radio was on. The Red Sox were playing the Cleveland Indians at Fenway Park, trailing by two runs in the bottom of the ninth inning.

One out, two runners on base.

David Ortiz at the dish.

Must we continue?

Ortiz socked a three-run, walkoff home run off a 22-year-old kid named Fausto Carmona to power the Sox to a thrilling 9-8 victory over the Indians, and that's when we said, "OK. Enough. We give up. We're convinced. Yes, yes, yes, David Ortiz is the greatest clutch hitter in Red Sox history."

Despite the frequent late-inning home runs by the beloved Boston sports icon known as Big Papi, this was not an easy decision. Again, we were stuffing ourselves with slices of Big Yaz Bread as we worked on this. The problem, though, is that Ortiz kept providing game-winning walkoff hits, so many that at one point Sox pitcher Curt Schilling told reporters, "You decide that it's mathematically impossible for him to do it again. But just as you say it, he does do it again."

Even before the 2006 season began, John H. Henry, the principal owner of the Red Sox, had given a plaque to Ortiz on which was written something along the lines of "David Ortiz: Greatest Clutch Hitter in Red Sox History." (And if Henry thinks he's getting a cut on sales of this book, he has another thing coming.) Anyway, Henry was basing his case on Big Papi's many great deeds before the 2006 season, including three extra-inning, walkoff postseason hits: his pennant-clinching home run off the Angels' Jarrod Washburn in the 10th inning of Game 3 of the Division Series, his 12th-inning homer to keep the Red Sox alive in Game 4 of the ALCS against the Yankees, and, the next night, his 14th-inning single in Game 5.

He is the only player in baseball history with three post-season walkoff hits.

Yet, we remained stubborn. We didn't want to overlook Yastrzemski, who in 1967 almost single-handedly carried the "Impossible Dream" Red Sox to the American League pennant. In the final two games of the '67 season, with the Sox needing to sweep the Minnesota Twins to keep their pennant hopes alive, Yaz went a combined 7-for-8 with six RBI, including a three-run homer.

True, Yaz popped out against Goose Gossage to end the Sox' playoff game against the Yankees in 1978. But he did drive in two of Boston's four runs that day, with a second-inning home run off Yankees starter Ron Guidry and an eighth-inning single off Gossage. And remember: Yaz was 39 years old at the time.

Peter Gammons of ESPN once made note of the 20 most important games of Yastrzemski's career. He included the two games against the Twins, the '78 game against the Yankees, and Yaz' 17 postseason games from 1967 and 1975. In those 20 games, Yaz hit .423 (33-for-78) with six home runs and 19 RBI.

But while Yastrzemski's contributions to the Red Sox must never be forgotten, Ortiz has taken his rightful place as the team's greatest clutch hitter. And as if his postseason contributions were not enough, Ortiz turned into a veritable Clutch Cargo in 2006: The July 31 home run to beat the Indians was, incredibly, his fifth walkoff hit of the season, and coming at a time when the Sox, as always, were battling the Yankees for first place in the American League East.

After his home run to beat the Indians, Ortiz said, "You gotta do what you gotta do, right?"

For Ortiz, right. For Yaz, right.

For pretty much everyone else, wrong.

WHO WAS THE GREATEST CLUTCH PERFORMER IN CELTICS HISTORY?

By the time the 1984-85 National Basketball Association season had arrived, the legend of Larry Bird had already been firmly established. He had led the Celtics to NBA championships in 1981 and '84, and by now he was being cited not just as one of history's great Celtics, but as one of the best players the game had ever seen.

He was also one of basketball's greatest clutch performers, which brings us to the '84-85 season. As the printed word fails to convey completely just how dynamic Bird could be in clutch situations—that's what highlight reels are for—it's best to offer a two-game snapshot.

Our saga begins on January 27, 1985, at the old Boston Garden. Bird scored 48 points that night, but it was his buzzer-beater that provided the winning margin in a 128-127 victory over the Portland Trailblazers.

Two nights later, the Celtics played another home game, only the "home" on this occasion was Hartford. In those days, the Celtics played a handful of each season's games at the Hartford Civic Center, an arrangement that nobody in uniform enjoyed. Bird would certainly fall into this category. He hated the nearly two-hour bus ride to Hartford.

A sellout crowd of 15,685 turned out on this night at the Hartford Civic Center, and, as he had done a couple of nights earlier in Boston, Bird again delivered victory. This time, his buzzer beater powered the Celtics to a 131-130 victory over the Detroit Pistons.

Looking back on those two games, many Celtics fans may have forgotten the scores, or the opponents, or, perhaps, that one of the two games was played not in Boston, but in Hartford. (Just as some have forgotten, or never knew, that it was at the Hershey Sports Arena in Hershey, Pennsylvania, that Wilt Chamberlain registered his 100-point game.)

What is remembered, though, is that in back-to-back games Larry Bird had accomplished every schoolboy's dream: the last-second, game-winning shot.

"More than anyone in the history of the Celtics," said Celtics play-by-play broadcaster Glenn Ordway, "the ball went to Larry when the game was on the line. Plays were designed for him. Everybody in the building, including the opposition, knew he was going to get the ball. And he was able to respond nine out of 10 times.

"Those people are special," said Ordway. "It's almost as if they've willed themselves, when they're going into the game, that they're going to make the shot at the end. It's like they play the entire game knowing that, in the end, they'll take the shot to win it."

If you believe that sounds trite, that it's one of those fill-in-the-name-of-star-athlete-here declarations, then, well, you never saw Larry Bird play.

As for those who did see the man play, and perform in the clutch, they surely have their personal favorites. Never to be left out, for instance, is Bird's steal of an Isiah Thomas inbounds pass in the waning seconds of a 1987 playoff game against the Pistons, followed by an over-the-shoulder pass to Dennis Johnson for the game-winning basket. It's one of the most talked-about plays in NBA history.

But those two January nights in 1987 alone create a highlight reel. Watch those two plays and you don't need to see anything more to understand what Larry Bird was all about.

105

DOES NANCY KERRIGAN OWE TONYA HARDING A THANK YOU? (NOT THAT TONYA SHOULD HOLD HER BREATH)

38 How can we possibly suggest such a horrible idea? In perhaps the worst act of unsportsmanlike conduct not involving George Steinbrenner, Tonya conspired to smash Nancy's knee with a tire iron barely a month before the 1994 Winter Olympics to guarantee herself a spot on the U.S. team. It took a U.S. figure skating loophole just to get Nancy on the Olympic team that year. Even then, the Stoneham, Massachusetts native's training was seriously cut back and she had to share ice time with a woman who should have been in the Corleone family instead of representing the United States in the Olympics.

So why does Nancy owe Tonya anything other than a slap in the face and a spit in the eye? Because Tonya made Nancy—and every other skater for the next decade—rich and famous.

Other than in years when a group of college hockey players are performing miracles, women's figure skating is usually the biggest event at the Winter Olympics, and the gold medalist becomes a national celebrity. But Tonya's crime elevated the event well beyond even that, turning it into the biggest sports story of the decade. The soap opera that pitted the New England gal against Oregon trailer trash turned figure skating into a national phenomenon, inspiring movies, books, made-for-TV competitions, ice shows, and even, shudder, skating fantasy leagues. More than a decade later, there was even an opera based on the Tonya-Nancy saga.

And contrary to popular opinion, the knee-capping did not necessarily cost Kerrigan the gold medal. While she was America's top medal candidate, Nancy was not favored to win at the Olympics even before the crime. Ukraine's Oksana Baiul was the reigning world champion, while France's Surya Bonaly had finished second at World's the previous two years. China's Lu Chen won the bronze at the world championships. And Nancy? She won the bronze at the '92 Olympics but finished a disappointing fifth at the '93 Worlds.

Nancy skated superbly in Lillehammer but was just eclipsed by Baiul, the 16-year-old orphan who overcame her own injury—the future star of "Celebrity Poker Showdown" won despite needing two painkilling shots for a back injury suffered during a collision with a skater the previous day (no, Baiul had not been drinking).

107

Normally, silver medalists do not become household names (quick—tell us who won the silver at Salt Lake in 2002 or Torino in 2006), but Nancy did because of everything that had happened. A dozen years after it all went down, she still was headlining skating shows and hosting golf tournaments, and was involved in charity work. Clearly, she earned much of that on her own hard work and talent. But her continuing fame is also due in large part to Tonya. Kerrigan may have famously cried, "Why me?" when she was hit, but we would have long since forgotten her had it not happened.

Of course, we understand if Nancy sees things a bit differently.

THE BOSTON SPORTS TRIVIA QUESTION THAT WON'T EVER GO AWAY

Every city has a collection of obscure, offbeat sports trivia questions that manage to get passed down through the generations, like grandpa's watch or a job at the state house. In Boston, two such questions are still making the rounds:

• Who is the only man to play for the Red Sox, Celtics, and Bruins?

• Who started at second base for the Red Sox on Opening Day in 1967?

Now before we begin the debate, it just makes sense to get the answers out of the way first. (If you grew up in Boston, chances are you already know. If you are not from Boston you no doubt are breathless with anticipation, so let's get to it.)

Both questions are of the "trick" variety. The only man to play for the Celtics, Bruins, and Red Sox? Why, that would be the late, great organist John Kiley, who for many years warmed up the pregame crowds at Fenway Park and the old Boston Garden, usually with such standards as "Everything's Coming up Roses," "Oklahoma," and other ditties from old Broadway musicals. Given his playbook, it's doubtful Kiley ever missed a performance of whatever Broadway musical that happened to be passing through Boston on its national tour.

As for the Red Sox' starting second baseman on Opening Day in 1967, the trick here is that the man who got the nod—and wound up starting the first six games of the '67 season at second base—was Reggie Smith, who became a mainstay in center field for the Red Sox for seven seasons, and then settled in as a right fielder the second half of his career with the Cardinals, Dodgers and, at the end, the Giants.

The Reggie Smith/second base question has stood the test of time for no other reason than because the '67 Red

109

Sox forever changed baseball in New England. Aging Red Sox fans would have you believe that Fenway Park has been filled for every game since it opened in 1912, but the reality is that, pre-1967, the Sox had played uninspired ball for most of the previous 20 seasons.

And so it is that, as fans look back on the "Impossible Dream" season of 1967, they lock onto certain events and won't ever let go of them. There's Bill Rohr's flirtation with a no-hitter against the Yankees in his first big-league start. Or the tragic August night when Tony Conigliaro was beaned by a Jack Hamilton pitch.

As for Smith playing second base, it was a stopgap measure by first-year Red Sox manager Dick Williams. He needed someone to mind the store until the injured Mike Andrews, yet another rookie, was ready to play every day. Come the seventh game of the season, Andrews started at second base, and Smith returned to center, where he would play 144 games in '67.

He never played another game at second base in his career, which lasted 17 years.

The question, then, is this: Which of these "trivia" questions is No. 1? It just makes sense to go with Kiley, since the answer always brings quizzical expressions to the faces of younger fans who didn't know what they were getting themselves into.

John Kiley, who died in 1993, would have loved it.

DID BOSTON FANS REALLY SUFFER MORE THAN EVERYONE ELSE?

40 This might come as a surprise to many Boston fans, but people outside Route 495 have had just about enough talk about how long the city suffered between Red Sox championships. And for good reason.

Yes, 86 years is a long time to wait for a championship (though it's about an average wait for the cable guy to finally show up). But how many Red Sox fans actually waited that long? You have to be in your 90s to have suffered throughout the entire World Series drought. The vast majority of Red Sox fans—and pretty much every fan who ever called into a talk radio show to moan about their fate—had been waiting less than 50 years, and many waited a lot less.

Look, you don't get extra credit for suffering because of what your old man and his father went through. That's like asking a college to grant you a degree because your dad had such a high GPA or petitioning for a Purple Heart because your grandfather was wounded on the beaches of Normandy.

The point is, if your team hasn't won in your lifetime, they might as well have never won. And once your lifetime gets beyond three and four decades, well, then you've paid some pretty serious dues. Millions of Red Sox fans fell into that category. But so do Cubs, Giants, Astros, Padres, Brewers, and Mariners fans. The Giants haven't won a World Series since they moved to San Francisco half a century ago. They lost the 1962 World Series to the Yankees when they had the winning run on second base in the bottom of the ninth inning of Game 7. They waited 27 years to get back and were hit by an earthquake midway through the series. They waited another 13 years and had a five-run lead with eight outs separating them from a world championship and they still lost.

The Astros have had it even worse. They lost a best-of-five playoff series in 1980 when four games went into extra innings and they went into the eighth inning of the final game with a lead and Nolan Ryan on the mound. They got knocked out of the 1986 playoffs with a 16-inning loss. They lost the 2004 NLCS despite leading the final game with Clemens on the mound. They finally reached the World Series after 43 years and got swept. And worst of all, they had to wear those hideous rainbow jerseys and play a cameo role in *Bad News Bears in Breaking Training*.

And don't even bring up the Cubs.

At least San Francisco and Houston, like Boston, have had championships to celebrate in other sports. Cleveland not only has endured the woeful Indians' drought for nearly 60 years, but also suffered through those miserable playoff losses to Michael Jordan and the Bulls and to John Elway and the Broncos. And they lost their football team on top of that.

So pardon if Cleveland fans don't want to hear about the agony of Boston fans, who have enjoyed nine NBA championships, three Super Bowl titles, two Stanley Cups and, finally, a World Series, since any team in their city last won something important. Trust us, they've had it much worse.

WHO WAS THE MOST IMPORTANT FRONT-OFFICE EXECUTIVE IN RED SOX HISTORY?

It always makes for delightful and entertaining reading when some baseball poet scribbles away about how, since the dawn of time, the Red Sox have had a magical hold on the hearts of New Englanders.

The problem, of course, is that it's not true. Following the 1919 season, when Babe Ruth was sold to the Yankees, the Red Sox were a laughingstock for most of the next 25 years, until winning a pennant in 1946. And it would take another 21 years before a new breed of Red Sox players fashioned their "Impossible Dream" season, capturing the 1967 American League pennant.

The architect of the '67 Red Sox—indeed, the man most responsible for the cultlike following the Sox enjoy today—is Dick O'Connell.

One of the key dates in Red Sox history is September 16, 1965, the day team owner Thomas Yawkey fired general manager Mike Higgins, a good old boy who never seemed bothered by the organization's inability to find room on their big-league roster for African American players. Worth noting is something else that happened that day: Dave Morehead, a 23-year-old right-hander, pitched a no-hitter against the Cleveland Indians. Attendance that day at Fenway Park was 1,247.

In 1965, the Red Sox drew only 652,201 fans to Fenway Park. Nobody cared about this team, and that was something O'Connell was going to change. What he had going for him was that Yawkey had grown disinterested in the team, rarely bothering to leave his South Carolina estate to monitor what was happening at Fenway Park. And so it was that O'Connell began staffing the roster with black players signed by the team's farm director, Neil Mahoney. By 1967, such young black players as Reggie Smith, Joe Foy, and George Scott were on the 25-man roster. As Glenn Stout and Richard A. Johnson have written in *Red Sox Century*, the definitive history of the franchise, "...under O'Connell and Neil Mahoney, Boston's increasingly colorblind farm system had never been more productive." And as O'Connell himself once said, "I don't care what color a player is as long as he can play."

O'Connell had no interest in causes. Nor was he trying to make a statement. He wanted to win, is all. It was in that spirit that he fired manager Billy Herman, placing the future of the club—and, by extension, his own future—in the hands of brash 35-year-old Dick Williams, who had been managing the team's Triple-A Toronto ballclub.

On Opening Day, 1967, only 8,324 fans turned out to see the Red Sox emerge with a 5-4 victory over the Chicago White Sox. But the summer of '67 produced a never-to-be-forgotten pennant race, and by the end of the season the Sox were packing Fenway Park.

It would be several more years before the Red Sox would move beyond the racial barriers that had been in place for decades, and another 27 years before the team would finally win a World Series. But Dick O'Connell had provided a blueprint to success.

And, given the franchise shifts that would soon take place in baseball—over the next few years the Milwaukee Braves, Washington Senators, and Kansas City Athletics would move to new cities—it's not implausible to suggest Dick O'Connell may have saved baseball in Boston.

SHOULD ROGER CLEMENS GO INTO COOPERSTOWN WEARING A RED SOX CAP?

42 The Pro Football Hall of Fame is boring. Inducted players aren't depicted wearing helmets, so there is never any spirited controversy over which team they should represent. Baseball is much better. Not only do we argue passionately over which players belong in Cooperstown, when we finally do agree on someone, we argue passionately over which cap he should wear on his Hall of Fame plaque.

Which brings us to Clemens, who has said several times that when he finally retires for good, he wants to go into the Hall wearing a Yankees cap. He's even threatened to boycott his induction if the Hall doesn't grant his wish.

The case for the Yankees is almost legitimate. Clemens won 77 games and his sixth Cy Young in New York; more importantly, he won his only two world championships there. That's impressive, but it ignores the fact that he spent only five of his 23 big league seasons in New York. That's barely adequate time to get a cab in the rain in New York, let alone overcome the case for Boston, where

Clemens was around nearly as long as the Big Dig.

The Red Sox are the team that originally signed Clemens in 1983. He spent the first 14 seasons of his professional career and the first 13 seasons of his big league career with the Red Sox. He set the record for most strikeouts in a game with Boston (and then matched it 10 years later). He won his first three Cy Young awards and his only MVP with Boston. He won more than half his games and registered more than half of his career strikeouts with Boston. He made almost half his All-Star appearances for the Red Sox. He was the best pitcher in Red Sox history.

This "I Want to Wear a Yankees Cap" nonsense all boils down to Clemens still holding a grudge against Dan Duquette for saying he was washed up after the 1996 season. But a player's feud with a former general manager is hardly sufficient reason for ignoring history.

The whole cap thing wasn't an issue until players started working out deals with teams to wear their cap in the Hall of Fame. Wade Boggs, who had nearly 2,100 of his hits for Boston and just 210 for the Devil Rays, tried to go into the Hall with a Tampa Bay cap. Gary Carter, like Clemens, requested that he go in wearing the team cap (Mets) with which he won the World Series. The Hall of Fame overruled both times, saying that it maintains the sole judgment for which cap a player wears on his plaque.

The Hall will do the same when the time comes for Clemens. And it should say he goes in with a B on his cap.

117

HAS JOHNNY PESKY BEEN UNFAIRLY MALIGNED FOR "HOLDING THE BALL" IN THE 1946 WORLD SERIES?

43 Johnny Pesky never grows tired of regaling listeners with the story about the Oregon-Oregon State football game he attended after the 1946 World Series. As Pesky will tell you, with great fervor, it was a lousy day for football, so rainy, so muddy, that fumbles were taking place with great frequency.

And so it was that a fan stood up, put hands to mouth, and hollered, "Give the ball to Pesky! He'll hold onto it!"

Pesky, who in 2006, approaching his 86th birthday, was still working for the Red Sox, insists the incident really did happen. But even if it's an urban legend, or an old banquet joke that has morphed into historical fact, it's in keeping with an actual event from the '46 World Series that has itself been transformed over the years.

The '46 Red Sox, winners of the American League pennant, battled the National League's St. Louis Cardinals to a deciding Game 7 in the World Series. In the bottom of the eighth inning at Sportsman's Park, the game tied 3-3, the

Cardinals' Enos "Country" Slaughter led off with a single to center. With two out, and with Slaughter running on the pitch, the Cardinals' Harry Walker lined a shot to left center.

Center fielder Leon Culberson came up with the ball and made a relay to Pesky, the shortstop, whose throw to the plate was too late to catch Slaughter, who had completed what came to be known as his "Mad Dash." The Red Sox were held scoreless in the ninth inning, preserving a 4-3 victory and a World Series championship for the Cardinals.

Those are the facts.

This is where the myth takes over. The story has been told, and likely will forever be told, that Pesky "held the ball," thereby allowing Slaughter to score the winning run. The story picked up steam in later years, with "Pesky held the ball" being placed alongside such Red Sox disasters as Joe McCarthy's decision to start journeyman Denny Galehouse in a 1948 playoff game against the Cleveland Indians, Bucky Dent's 1978 playoff home run off Mike Torrez, and, of course, the ball that went between Bill Buckner's legs in Game 6 of the 1986 World Series.

But, as is often the case with legends, urban or otherwise, certain facts are omitted for no other reason than because they ruin the fun. Take, for instance, the fact that Leon Culberson was in the game at all. A part-time player during his five seasons with the Red Sox, he had entered the game in the top of the eighth inning as a pinch-runner

119

for center fielder Dom DiMaggio, who had suffered a leg injury while running out a double to right.

Surviving footage of the play shows a not-so-strong throw to Pesky from shallow center field, leading to endless speculation that DiMaggio, were he in center, would have made a better throw to Pesky—or, better yet, thrown home. Though footage does not show Pesky "holding the ball," it does portray the shortstop as greatly surprised that Slaughter, at this point, had already rounded third. Pesky's throw was not a good one, but, even so, Slaughter was going to score.

What happened here is that Slaughter made one of the great plays in World Series history. But as blame must always be assessed, especially in Boston, it was handed to Pesky.

For that reason alone, nobody was happier when the Red Sox won the 2004 World Series . . . in St. Louis, of all places, and with Pesky on hand to see it happen.

SHOULD THE RED SOX TRADE MANNY?

We all work with people who can be a pain in the ass—guys who are always bitching about the lousy pay or the cramped cubicles or the poor array of snacks in the vending machines.

They're always threatening to finally take their "friend" up on that great job offer at a rival company for tons more money. But there never is a "great job offer." No one likes these people because they are never happy.

Which brings us to Manny Ramirez.

Manny is one of the most dangerous, productive hitters of his generation. At last glance, he had averaged 41 home runs, 130 RBIs, and 106 runs a season for the previous eight years. He had made eight consecutive All-Star Games and finished no lower than ninth in the MVP voting each of those seasons. He was the 2004 World Series MVP. He's a probable Hall of Famer.

He even occasionally catches some fly balls.

But, like our disgruntled co-worker, he's never happy. If he isn't bitching to his teammates or the front office that he wants to be traded, he's skipping out of a game so he can go have dinner with a rival player and bitch to him that he wants to be traded.

In most circumstances, we'd say, "Fine, good luck to you. Enjoy playing in Kansas City." But you can't do that with Manny. The only way a trade makes sense is if the Red Sox are better off after the deal, which seems pretty unlikely in this case.

For one thing, he still had two years remaining on his $160 million contract (plus two option years), the second-richest in baseball history, which severely limits the number of teams willing to make an offer. And even the few

121

teams who could afford his contract aren't eager to trade for an indifferent outfielder with a bad glove who occasionally loses count of outs. Hell, no team even claimed him when the Red Sox put him on irrevocable waivers after the 2003 season.

In other words, the Red Sox aren't going to get nearly enough in return if they trade him. Manny may be difficult, but he's still one of the game's best hitters. And given that he spends most of the game standing by himself in left field or alone in the batters box, the Red Sox really don't have to deal with him much other than counting up his home runs and RBIs.

Sure, it's great to have happy employees who love where they work, get along with all their co-workers, and volunteer to run the company softball team. But given the choice between a popular .260 hitter who donates his salary to the Jimmy Fund and a guy who hits .320 with 40 home runs and 125 RBIs, well, we'll take the slugger every time.

WHY "THE CURSE" IS THE BIGGEST JOKE IN THE HISTORY OF THE UNIVERSE

 The Curse of the Bambino, written by *Boston Globe* sports columnist Dan Shaughnessy, is a must-read for all Red Sox fans. Intended as a chronicle of the many horrific failures and collapses suffered by the Red Sox over the years, the book is rich with anecdotes and player recollections, and veers off on all kinds of humorous tangents, as when Shaughnessy, writing about the 1967 World Series, notes that ". . . *Housewives on Call* and *Tortured Females* played at the X-rated Mayflower Theatre, but manager Charlie Schultz said that there were few who gave in to temptation during World Series games."

But long, long after the book had faded into the past, with Shaughnessy moving on to other projects, it is the title of the book, with its suggestion that Babe Ruth placed a curse on the Red Sox after being sold to the New York Yankees, that took on a life its own.

123

The premise, based on a quick read of each year's final baseball standings from the time Ruth was sent packing, is really very simple: The Yankees, with their Bambino leading the way, went on to become one of the great dynasties in sports history, whereas the Red Sox, sans Ruth, spent most of the next 25 years as one of the game's laughingstock franchises.

Ruth, as the title implies, forever doomed the Red Sox to misery by placing some kind of "curse" on the team. And, as Shaughnessy points out, examples of the curse are everywhere: Former Red Sox pitcher Bruce Hurst, Boston's starter against the Mets in Game 7 of the 1986 World Series, is an anagram for B. Ruth Curse.

Don't blame Shaughnessy for any of this. It was a nice gimmick. It was catchy. It caught on. But once the national media dug its claws into the curse, insanity ruled. Dim-bulb reporters and gullible TV talking heads would traipse through Boston, asking passersby if they "really believe" in the curse, and, if so, would they be so kind as to share a story about, say, a dead grandfather who went bitterly to his grave because Joe McCarthy started Denny Galehouse in the 1948 playoff game against the Indians. Presented with the opportunity to be seen on television, or to be quoted in some far-away newspaper—"Hey, Sully, I'm gonna be in the Kansas City Star!"—many Sox fans couldn't resist.

Here's the problem: Being sold to the Yankees was the

greatest break of Ruth's life. In Boston, he was a pitcher and sometimes outfielder; in New York, having been turned loose as an everyday hitter, he made the home run his personal calling card.

In New York, Babe Ruth became a star of epic proportions. Not merely the most famous athlete in America, he became one of the most famous, most photographed men in the world, on a par with silent film stars Charlie Chaplin and Douglas Fairbanks.

He was well-compensated for his efforts. And, one assumes, the ever-social Babe met the acquaintance of a greater quantity (and quality?) of women than had he remained with the Red Sox.

To this day, the very name—Babe Ruth—is a synonym for greatness. When one speaks of the Babe Ruth of car salesmen or dental hygienists, or says that a drive from the 18th tee was of Ruthian proportions, even non-sports fans understand the meaning.

Babe Ruth's name will live forever. Wherever he is, it doesn't make sense that he'd be cursing the team that made it all possible.

THE MOST OVERRATED CLOSER IN RED SOX HISTORY

46 Tom Gordon once was so highly regarded that Stephen King wrote a book in which a lost girl is able to keep her wits about her thanks to the then Red Sox closer. His arm naturally, almost immediately turned to spaghetti. But he isn't the most overrated closer in Red Sox history.

It's bad enough that tourists still crowd the sidewalks on Beacon Street to gawk at the Bull & Finch Pub and Bostonians still have to listen to lame Cliff Claven jokes and other tired references to a sitcom that's been off the air (but not out of syndication) for 13 years. What's worse is that if you asked people outside Boston to name a Boston reliever, many will probably say Sam Malone before anyone else. It's sad. Everybody knows his name even if they don't have the slightest idea what a save situation is.

It's nonsense. You can look it up. Sam Malone never saved a single game for the Red Sox. It must have been like when Boston went with a closer by committee in 2003.

Sure, Malone had potential—haven't we heard that too many times about Boston pitchers?—but he couldn't overcome his considerable control problems on and off the field. "Sam and Eddie LeBec often closed down Daisy Buchanan's many nights," longtime Boston waitress Carla Tortelli said. "Actually, I believe Sam also opened Daisy's up the next morning."

The only reason Malone was ever on the Red Sox roster is because he was a family friend of mayor Frank Skeffington and because manager Don Zimmer was desperate for arms, any arms, after blowing out his staff midway through the 1978 season. But you still won't find Malone's name in the *Baseball Encyclopedia* because he never got into a single game. With the possible exception of Mickey Mantle, Malone was the only player in baseball history who went on the disabled list with cirrhosis of the liver.

"I remember one day I was examining his x-rays," said Dr. Daniel Auschlander, liver specialist at Boston's St. Eligius hospital, "and I was saying that due to the riddled organ and the leaking blood vessels and the damaged nerves he didn't have more than six months to live. Then Donald Westphal pointed out that I was actually looking at architectural plans for the Big Dig.

"But the thing is, Sam's liver was in such bad shape you honestly couldn't tell the difference."

Malone's Red Sox career ended after the 1981 strike when both the Red Sox and the players union neglected to tell him the strike was over. And he was too busy fighting off paternity suits to pay attention himself.

Attorney Denny Crane of the legal firm Crane, Poole, and Schmidt estimates he represented Malone in "13 or 15" of his paternity suits. "People think Sammy got the nickname 'May Day' because the Red Sox called for him when they were in distress," he said. "That wasn't it at all. It was because he kept calling the Red Sox front office and crying 'May Day' whenever the cops picked him up on a drunk and disorderly charge."

Meanwhile, who was the most underrated closer in Boston history? That's easy. It's also the best closer in Red Sox history, Dick Radatz. Forget Keith Foulke, Sparky Lyle, Lee Smith, Bob Stanley, and Schiraldi (please forget Schiraldi). Back when closers still had to work for a living, The Monster averaged 12 wins and 25 saves a season from 1962-65, never throwing less than 124 innings while averaging more than a strikeout an inning. In 1964 he went 16-9 with 29 saves, a 2.29 ERA and 181 strikeouts. Take that, Mariano.

WHO WERE THE THREE MOST IMPORTANT MEN IN THE HISTORY OF THE PATRIOTS?

What's that? A list of superlatives regarding the New England Patriots that does not include Tom Brady and Bill Belichick?

Such blasphemy! But while the Patriots would win three Super Bowl championships in four years under Belichick's coaching and Brady's quarterbacking, it is important to keep in mind that, by the time they arrived, this onetime laughingstock of a franchise had already been cemented as a New England institution.

Yes, Belichick will one day be enshrined in the Pro Football Hall of Fame, as will Brady. But in terms of taking the Pats from little more than an afterthought in the eyes of New England sports fans and turning them into a team with an almost cultlike following, three men deserve statues along Route 1:

Team owner Robert Kraft.

Coach Bill Parcells.

And, yes, Drew Bledsoe, who happened to be the Pats' quarterback in the days before Tom Brady.

Not counting Parcells' season as a linebackers coach in 1980, these men arrived in Foxboro at around the same time. Parcells, who had coached the New York Giants to two Super Bowl titles, was hired as the Pats' head coach on January 21, 1993, by then-owner James B. Orthwein. A little more than three months later, the Pats selected Bledsoe as the No. 1 pick in the draft. And exactly one year after Parcells had been hired, Robert Kraft, a local businessman and longtime Patriots season-ticket holder, purchased the team from Orthwein.

The building blocks were now in place. In Parcells, the Patriots had a head coach who could do more than talk about getting to the Super Bowl. He'd been there. In Bledsoe, the Pats had an exciting young (albeit not very mobile) quarterback who would lead the offense for the next eight seasons. And, most importantly, Kraft provided hope that the Patriots, forever rumored to be going the way of the Baltimore Colts, Los Angeles Rams, and the original Cleveland Browns—that is, spirited away to another city— would become a permanent fixture in New England.

It took Parcells exactly two seasons to coach the Patriots to a playoff berth. After an off-season in 1995 in which the Pats slumped to 6-10, they went on a tear the second half of the 1996 season and wound up playing the Green Bay Packers in Super Bowl XXXI, losing 35-21. (More about that, and about Parcells, in the next chapter.)

Bledsoe was a Pro Bowl selection in three of his first four seasons in the NFL. In the Super Bowl season of '96, he completed 373 of 623 passes for 4,086 yards and 27 touchdowns; his quarterback rating in '96 was 83.7, the highest of his career.

And, by now, people wanted to watch the Patriots. The team was routinely selling out home games, and the Kraft family, after 1) turning down several offers to sell the team and be done with the business of football, and 2) deciding against a plan to move the Patriots to Connecticut, announced plans to build a new, privately financed stadium next to Foxboro Stadium.

But while the Kraft family built the stadium, Parcells and Bledsoe built the interest that made it feasible.

... AND HOW ONE OF THOSE MEN COUGHED UP A SUPER BOWL-SIZED FURBALL

Of the work Bill Parcells did during the regular season with the 1996 Patriots there is no debate. The man bullied, cajoled, inspired, and masterminded his players to an 11-5 record, followed by playoff victories over the Pittsburgh Steelers and Jacksonville Jaguars.

It was when the Patriots arrived in New Orleans to prepare for Super Bowl XXXI against the Green Bay Packers that Parcells stopped devoting 100 percent of his time to coaching . . . and started dialing for dollars. He had already turned Super Bowl Week into the Bill Parcells Show by confiding to *Boston Globe* columnist Will McDonough that this would be his last season as coach of the Pats, after which the Tuna held a laughable press conference during which he claimed he had no knowledge of the story.

Perhaps Parcells didn't see the actual story because he was too busy lining up his new job as head coach of the New York Jets. His relationship with Patriots owner Robert Kraft in shambles, Parcells simply shopped around for a new job—and never mind that he was still under contract to the Patriots, or that he was supposed to be looking for ways to beat the Packers.

The Pats wound up losing Super Bowl XXXI by a 35-21 score. The Pats put up the good fight, closing to within 27-21 on a Curtis Martin 18-yard touchdown run in the third quarter, but this was followed by disaster: The Packers' Desmond Howard took the ensuing kick and raced 99 yards for a touchdown.

When the game was over, Parcells didn't even return to New England with the team. He would later emerge as a "consultant" with the Jets, with Bill Belichick brought along as the nominal head coach. After a dog-and-pony press conference at the Jets' offices in Hempstead, New York, a deal between the two teams was struck that allowed Parcells to be named head coach, with Belichick being retooled as assistant head coach.

The question will forever be debated: Did Parcells devote all his energies to beating the Packers ... or was he too busy talking with the Jets? His supporters point to a man who is meticulous in his game preparation, a man who would never, ever fail to deliver the goods, especially with a Super Bowl at stake. But the Patriots have always claimed that telephone records leave a paper trail of communications between Parcells and the Jets, as has been addressed by Michael Holley in *Patriot Reign*, quite simply the best book ever written about the franchise.

Among many other revelations in Holley's book is this: Even Belichick, who would eventually extract himself from Parcells and return to New England to coach the Patriots, was critical of the Tuna's antics during Super Bowl Week.

"I can tell you firsthand, there was a lot of stuff going on prior to the game," Belichick told Holley. "I mean, him talking to other teams. He was trying to make up his mind about what he wanted to do. Which, honestly, I felt totally inappropriate. How many chances do you get to play for the Super Bowl? Tell them to get back to you in a couple of days. I'm not saying it was disrespectful to me, but it was in terms of the overall commitment to the team."

Did Parcells' job-hunting absolutely cost the Pats a Super Bowl? Again, the debate continues. What is clear is

133

that winning the game was not the only thing on his mind that week.

DID DON ZIMMER HAVE IT COMING?

 Fans outside Boston—and some in Boston as well—were appalled when Pedro Martinez tossed Don Zimmer to the ground during the Game 3 fight in the 2003 ALCS. How could Pedro throw a 72-year-old man to the ground? It's bad enough that Pedro throws at hitters and then ducks into the dugout whenever they want to retaliate. But to shove an elderly man to the ground so hard he wound up in the hospital? Did he have no sense of decency? Is there no level to which he wouldn't stoop? Did the Yankees need to hire security guards for Bob Sheppard for Pedro's next start in Yankee Stadium?

The anguished calls for Pedro's ejection/suspension/ extreme rendition would have been quite understandable except for one thing. He didn't do anything wrong.

Put yourself in Pedro's place. You've sparked a near riot by hitting one of the Yankees with a pitch. So far, so good, right? Now, you're standing in the dugout an inning later, watching Clemens zip a too-close pitch to Manny Ramirez.

Manny, being Manny, overreacts and challenges Clemens. The dugouts empty and suddenly this 72-year-old coach is charging across the field as if he's an angry Doberman and you're wearing a top sirloin jersey.

It's a no-win situation. You can't fight Zimmer, because that would be beating up a man drawing social security. You can't let him hit you, either, because as old as he is, he's got enough steam going to seriously injure you and knock you out of the most important game of the year. And that head of his is damn solid.

Pedro did about the only thing he could. He ducked out of the way and reached out for Zimmer's head—it's hard to miss, really—to stop him. The momentum carried Zimmer to the ground, producing one of the oddest quotes in post-season history from Clemens: "Andy Pettitte and I went over there and I saw a bald head on the ground. We weren't sure if it was Zim or David Wells."

"It was kind of funny," Boston reliever Scott Sauerbeck said. "It reminded me of when Tommy Lasorda fell down during the All-Star Game. Zim hit the ground and he just kept rolling. It looked like he was rolling downhill. We thought he was going to roll into the dugout."

Zimmer wound up in the hospital as a precaution, but the only injuries he suffered were to his pride. He publicly apologized the next day, saying he was out of line.

And he *was* in the wrong. There is no excuse for any coach—72 years old or otherwise—to charge out of the

135

dugout and attack an opponent. Pedro may have been portrayed as the bad guy, but he did the right thing. As Sauberbeck said, "I don't care if the guy is in a wheelchair, you have to defend yourself."

Zimmer had it coming to him. And we're not just saying that because he was wearing a Yankees uniform or that he blew that big lead in 1978. Although neither of those things help.

WHO WAS BOSTON'S GREATEST OWNER?

50 Ask 1,000 Boston sports fans to name the greatest owner in Boston sports history, and 996 of them will fire back with Robert Kraft, who transformed the Patriots into a slick, smooth-running operation, from the three Super Bowl championships in four years to the gleaming new stadium on Route 1.

But while Kraft's work established the Patriots as a player in the New England sports market, challenging the Red Sox for the hearts, minds, and dollars of a passionate fan base, he wasn't pushing his rent money to the middle of the table to meet the payroll.

No, that honor would go to Walter Brown, the original owner of the Celtics.

Brown was never a wealthy man, not one of the so-called "sportsman owners" of yesteryear. He was a career behind-the-scenes man, an operator who did what he could to get things done. He was running the old Boston Garden—as had his father before him—when he helped establish the Basketball Association of America, emerging as founder of a modest little troupe of hoopsters he christened the Celtics.

The Celtics posted losing records their first four seasons. Brown hired Arnold "Red" Auerbach as coach beginning with the 1950-51 season. Sure, the Celtics went on to become famously successful, but even then Brown was often forced to extreme measures to make it all work. He once took out a second mortgage on his house to pay his players their playoff shares.

In addition to running the Celtics, and running the Boston Garden, Brown also took over the presidency of the struggling Boston Bruins in 1951 and brought order to the franchise.

"He did the job that, today, three different people are being paid very handsomely to do," says Dick Johnson, curator of the Sports Museum of New England.

In addition to many other pursuits—he coached an amateur hockey club, the Boston Olympics, to five national titles—Brown was also a co-founder of the Ice Capades, which helped Auerbach make a remarkably shrewd trade: To inspire the Rochester Royals to bypass Bill Russell with their No. 1 overall pick in the 1956 draft, Brown supplied some choice appearances by the Ice Capades for the good people of Rochester. Then, when the St. Louis Hawks selected Russell with the No. 2 pick, they shipped him to Boston for Easy Ed Macauley and the rights to Cliff Hagan.

Considering the Celtics would win 11 of the next 13 NBA championships, it was quite a deal.

Yet it was not Brown's most important contribution to the history of the Celtics.

In 1950, against the wishes of some owners, the Celtics became the first team to draft an African American player when Brown selected 6'5", 210-pound forward Chuck Cooper in the second round. According to writer George Sullivan in his definitive book on the team's early years, *The Picture History of the Boston Celtics*, Brown, a visionary, made the following announcement in selecting Cooper: "I don't give a damn if he's striped or polka dot or plaid. Boston takes Charles Cooper of Duquesne."

Cooper went on to play four seasons with the Celtics and then finished out his career with the Milwaukee Hawks and Fort Wayne Pistons.

Brown, who died in 1964, was inducted into the Hockey Hall of Fame in 1962, and, posthumously, to the Basketball Hall of Fame in 1965.

Of the plethora of uniform numbers retired by the Celtics

over the years, there is no debate over the No. 1 that hangs from the Garden rafters. It's in honor of Walter Brown.

WHO IS THE SECOND BEST HITTER IN RED SOX HISTORY?

If you need us to name the best hitter in Red Sox history, put this book down now, pick up your dog-eared copy of *The Lord of the Rings*, and return to your bedroom in your parents' basement because there is absolutely no hope for you. Meanwhile, we'll try and figure out the best Boston hitter not named Ted Williams.

In order to establish a minimum standard of Boston longevity, we decided to limit this question to players with at least 10 full seasons in a Red Sox uniform, which leaves three prime candidates: Jim Rice, Wade Boggs, and Carl Yastrzemski.

For just about a decade, there was no more feared batter in all baseball than Rice. In these days of inflated statistics it's difficult to recall just how impressive his 1978 season was—.315, 46 HR, 139 RBIs, 121 runs. For crying out loud, Rice once snapped a bat in half just checking his swing. But he also struck out a lot, didn't walk very much, grounded into 315 double plays, and got old overnight at age 34.

There are a couple things everyone knows for certain about Boggs. That he led the league in batting five times. That he was so superstitious he ate chicken before every game. That he had an affair with Margo Adams. And that he was nothing but a banjo hitter. Well, the first three are accurate but the fourth is not. True, Boggs didn't hit many home runs—he only once hit more than eight in a season— but that doesn't mean he didn't have any power. He was almost always in the top three in doubles, which, coupled with his singles and walks, usually put him among the leaders in OPS. In fact, he led the league twice in OPS, which is the best overall measure of a batter's perform- ance. And true, he only once drove in as many as 80 runs. But that wasn't his job. His job was to get on base and set the table for others. And he did it beautifully, scoring 100 runs seven times. The only drawback to Boggs' claim as Boston's second best hitter is that his final 912 hits and last five .300 seasons came in a different uniform.

Yaz has many things in his favor. He played his entire career in Boston, stepping to the plate nearly 14,000 times, reaching safely almost 5,300 times, and rounding the bases with a home run 452 times. He led the league in bat- ting three times, in OPS four times, and in on-base per- centage five times. He is the last batter to win the Triple Crown. On the other hand, he finished with a .285 career average (43 points lower than Boggs), had just four sea- sons in which he hit as many as 25 home runs (a total

Manny usually has by the All-Star break), and had twice as many seasons with less than 75 RBIs than he did with more than 100 RBIs. From 1971 on—the final 12 seasons of his career—he wasn't much more than a mediocre hitter.

So, who is the second best hitter in Red Sox history? From the point of pure hitting and consistency, we say Boggs. Barely. And only on days he had extra helpings of chicken.

WHAT WAS THE GREATEST DRAFT IN BOSTON SPORTS HISTORY?

When the New England Patriots selected Tom Brady in the sixth round of the 2000 National Football League draft, they landed themselves a quarterback who would go on to lead the team to three Super Bowl championships in four years. And counting.

In 1976, the Pats landed a future Hall of Famer in cornerback Mike Haynes, along with center Pete Brock and defensive back Tim Fox, each of whom blossomed into stars with the team. In 1995, the Pats had another star-studded draft, selecting cornerback Ty Law, linebacker Ted Johnson, running back Curtis Martin (a third-round steal), cornerback Jimmy Hitchcock, and center Dave Wohlabaugh. They would play a combined 397 games for the Patriots, with Law (four) and Martin (two) combining for six Pro-Bowl selections.

In 1983, a University of Texas fireballer named Roger Clemens was inexplicably left unselected for the first 18 picks of baseball's amateur draft. Clemens, who went to the Red Sox on pick No. 19, would spend 13 seasons with the Red Sox, winning 192 games, tying him with Cy Young for the franchise record for victories by a pitcher.

But while Brady and Clemens are among the greatest individual draftees in Boston sports history, and while the Pats have had some memorable days in what the NFL people like to call "The War Room," no general manager ever had a better draft than did the Celtics' Red Auerbach in 1956.

Did the Pats land a future Hall of Famer when they drafted Brady? Yes. Did the Sox land a future Hall of Famer when they drafted Clemens? Of course. But what Auerbach accomplished in 1956 is otherworldly. By coming away from the draft table with Bill Russell, Tommy Heinsohn, and K. C. Jones, the Celtics had selected three Hall of Famers.

Russell, of course, was the crown jewel, the greatest draft in sports history. The Celtics actually traded two players (Easy Ed Macauley and the rights to Cliff Hagan) to the St. Louis Hawks in order to get the pick needed to land Russell, a 6'10" center from the University of San Francisco. And, as we have seen, it didn't hurt that Celtics owner Walter Brown offered some choice Ice Capades dates to the good people of Rochester to help inspire the Rochester Royals to bypass Russell with their No. 1 overall pick in the draft.

The Celtics then used their own first-round selection for a "territorial pick" that landed Heinsohn, a star at the University of Holy Cross in nearby Worcester. With their second-round pick, the Celtics selected Russell's USF teammate, K. C. Jones, and then waited a couple of years for Jones to serve a hitch in the Army and to complete his flirtation with playing football for the Los Angeles Rams.

Russell and Heinsohn helped lead the Celtics to their first NBA title. Beginning in 1957, Russell, Heinsohn, and Jones played on eight consecutive Celtics championship teams.

Russell entered the Hall of Fame in 1974. Heinsohn was enshrined in 1986, followed by Jones in 1989.

WHAT WAS THE WORST DRAFT IN BOSTON SPORTS HISTORY?

Just so we're clear on this, even the Boston Celtics—and even with the great Red Auerbach at the controls—had some bad drafts. Scroll through the list of first-round

Celtics draft picks over the years and you'll be introduced to the likes of Clarence Glover, Steve Downing, and Michael Smith.

And while recognizing that Major League Baseball's amateur draft is something of a crap shoot, the Red Sox have made first-round picks out of such long-forgotten souls as Noel Jenke, Joel Bishop, Eddie Ford, Otis Foster, Dan Gabriele, and Tom Fischer.

But in terms of a) expectations and b) delivery on those expectations, the 1997 New England Patriots stand alone as the architects of the worst draft in Boston sports history.

It is important to note the role Bill Parcells played in giving the Patriots and their fans so much anticipation going into the '97 draft. Parcells, remember, had bolted the Patriots after Super Bowl XXXI to become head coach of the Jets, who were then forced to hand over to the Pats an array of draft picks as compensation.

Two of those picks were put into play in the 1997 draft, and Pats fans were jubilant: Not only would the Pats use their own picks to add depth to an already strong team, but those extra picks from the Jets would add yet more talent.

Thanks, Tuna!

Alas, it didn't turn out that way. Led by Bobby Grier, the team's vice president in charge of player personnel, the Patriots not only failed to add depth to the roster for the upcoming season, but did nothing to build for the future.

Their first-round pick, defensive back Chris Canty of

Kansas State, surely looked the part of a big-time NFL star. Alas, he was all hot dog—the kind of player who'd make a crushing tackle after a wideout had made a 19-yard reception and then start strutting up and down the field as though he'd just saved the season.

Canty played parts of just two seasons with the Patriots, starting only 10 games.

Defensive end Brandon Mitchell of Texas A&M, the team's second pick, did manage to hang on for five seasons with the Pats. But with their first compensation pick from the Jets, the Patriots reached out for Iowa running back Sedrick Shaw, who lasted two seasons, starting just one game. If you heard Shaw's name at all during a Patriots game, it was usually accompanied by the words, "Loss of three."

The Pats' other compensation pick from the Jets that year, in the fourth round, was used to select linebacker Damon Denson of Michigan. He played parts of three seasons, starting four games. Other picks by the Patriots in the 1997 draft include defensive back Chris Carter of Texas in the third round. He played parts of three seasons, starting 15 games. Linebacker Ed Ellis of Buffalo, taken in the fourth round, played parts of three seasons, starting one game. With linebacker Vernon Crawford of Florida State, a fifth-round pick, it was the same thing: parts of three seasons, one start.

Sixth-round pick Tony Gaiter of the University of Miami appeared in one game over two seasons. Seventh-round pick Scott Rehberg, a linebacker from Central Michigan, appeared in eight games over two seasons.

Bobby Grier was fired following the 1999 season.

WHAT WAS THE MOST MEMORABLE PITCH IN FENWAY HISTORY?

54 The Fenway Park mound. Where Smoky Joe Wood outdueled Walter Johnson 1-0 in 1912. Where the Babe threw the first pitch of his major-league career. Where Ernie Shore pitched a perfect game in relief. Where Clemens set the major league record for most strikeouts in a game. Where Pedro knocked down Karim Garcia. And where pitchers threw more than 1.5 million other balls and strikes over the past nine decades.

But the most memorable pitch of them wasn't thrown by a pitcher and it wasn't even thrown in a game. That's because the most memorable pitch in Fenway history was thrown by Ted Williams before the 1999 All-Star Game.

Williams was 80 years old and would be dead within three years. He was crippled by two strokes and a broken hip. He couldn't even walk to the mound, relying instead on a golf cart. He was so weak and his vision was so bad that Tony Gwynn needed to steady his hand and point out his honorary catcher, Carlton Fisk. The pitch had so little velocity that as a friend once wrote, you didn't need a speed gun to measure it, you just needed to count "One Mississippi, two Mississippi."

None of that mattered. Because when he was introduced as "The Greatest Hitter Who Ever Lived," Williams became The Kid all over again. It's said there is no crying in baseball, but there was that evening. Throats formed lumps so large it looked as if everyone had swallowed baseballs. And that wasn't the fans; that was the players, including 31 members of the All-Century team in addition to the 1999 All-Stars.

Almost none of those '99 All-Stars was alive when Williams played his final game. They knew him the way most of us know him—through a few film clips, the stories we've heard, and the almost unbelievable numbers on the back of his baseball card. Yet these millionaire major leaguers spontaneously swarmed around Ted as if they were little kids begging for an autograph. They were so overwhelmed by the moment the p.a. announcer had to request that they clear the field and play the game.

Never has a pregame moment so upstaged everything that happened afterward. Throwing mid-90s fastballs and his baffling changeup, Pedro struck out the side in the first inning and two more in the second on 28 total pitches but his performance was completely overshadowed by Ted lobbing a single pitch.

147

"I thought the stadium was going down," Pedro told reporters afterward of the ovation for Ted. "I don't think that there will be any other man that's going to replace that one."

No one who was there that evening will ever forget it. The only way it could have been more emotional is if Ted had walked out of a cornfield.

BOSTON: FOOTBALL TOWN OR BASEBALL TOWN?

 Yes, a case can be made that Boston is a "football town."

The problem is, the people who write great essays in support of this argument have been doing so with crayons, their words printed unsteadily on the sides of old paper bags.

Either that, or they moved to Boston a few years ago, noted the increased popularity of the New England Patriots, and then trucked out the ever-handy, "Boston is now a football town." This is usually accompanied by the bold pronouncement that "football is the new national pastime," and that baseball "is dead."

OK. Let's proceed . . . very . . . slowly. Football is not the new national pastime. Has it become the most popular sport in America? Yes. Does it get higher television ratings than baseball? Absolutely. But let's remember that the term "national pastime" harkens back to an era when baseball was virtually the only team sport being played in the United States; its first known usage, according to *The Dickson Baseball Dictionary*, can be traced to 1857.

In the 21st century, with the rise of NASCAR, the NBA, the internet, and cable television packages that include hundreds of niche stations, there is no such thing as a "national pastime." So let's be done with that argument.

While football has certainly supplanted baseball as the game of choice in many American cities, Boston is not one of them. And the Patriots, with their dazzling new stadium and three Super Bowl championships over four years, have absolutely passed the Bruins and Celtics and, in doing so, have closed in on the Red Sox.

But during the time the Pats became a football dynasty, the Red Sox, under new ownership, hit upon the idea that simply opening the gates to Fenway Park on game days was not in keeping with modern-day marketing techniques. Instead, the old ballpark was cleaned up, renovated, and expanded, and its team-owned television wing, NESN, was given a bold new look. It didn't hurt that, in 2004, the Red Sox won their first World Series in 86 years.

Beginning in 2003, the Red Sox began to routinely sell out every home game. Such is their popularity that, these days, thousands of Red Sox fans make pilgrimages to such cities as St. Petersburg, Baltimore, and Anaheim to see their team play on the road.

The football people will tell you that, when the Pats and Red Sox play head to head, the Patriots get the higher ratings. Well, of course: The Patriots play one game a week; baseball, as if this needs explaining, is an ever-evolving drama that plays out practically every night over the course of a six-month season.

It should be noted that Gerry Callahan, a *Boston Herald* columnist and morning talk-show show host at all-sports WEEI, and the city's leading advocate of the this-is-a-football-town argument, was asked, in June 2006, the following question: If you had to pick one team, either the Red Sox or Patriots, to move to California, which team that would it be?

He chose to send the Patriots out west, stating that he could still watch the games on television.

In other words, even the football guy needs to have the Red Sox around.

DID MILITARY SERVICE COST TED WILLIAMS THE HOME RUN RECORD?

56 In this era of the all-volunteer army, when the only people asked to make sacrifices during a war are the soldiers who volunteered for it and the families they left behind, it bears reminding that there was a time when everyone was expected to pitch in rather than get a cushy reserve job back in the states or a college deferment. Back then, you didn't get a $2 million signing bonus in the draft, you got $50 a month and a ticket to basic training.

At least 500 major leaguers served in World War II. At least 120 served in the military during the Korean War. And Ted Williams served in both. He missed almost five entire seasons to military service.

What records did that cost him? We'll never know for sure, but in 1942, Ted's last season before becoming a naval flyer, he won the Triple Crown with 36 home runs, 137 RBIs, and a .356 average. When he returned from the war in 1946, he hit .342 with 38 home runs and 123 RBIs. Six years later, when the government called him up again, Ted was coming off a season in which he hit .318 with 30 home runs and 126

RBIs. When he returned—after flying 39 missions—nearly dying in one—he homered in his second at-bat and then hit 41 more homers in his first 154 games back.

In all, Ted missed 727 games due to both wars, all of them during what should have been the most productive seasons of his career. He averaged roughly one home run in every four games from 1941 to 1954. Would he have been healthy enough to play every one of those games he missed? Probably not, though Ted did occasionally play every game at that stage of his career. Would he have averaged more home runs, though, had it not been for the disruptions? Maybe. (You try getting your swing back after three years). Would he have perhaps averaged more had he been able to play at age 24, 25, 26? Again, we'll never know. But it's not unreasonable to say that he would.

So let's give him 180 more home runs. That puts him at 701, still 13 shy of Ruth's record. But recall that Williams retired shortly after his 42nd birthday in 1960, despite hitting .316 with 29 home runs. He wasn't done by any stretch. Given that Ted's stated goal was always to be referred to as the greatest hitter who ever lived, it's a fair assumption that he would have played another season if he was within sight of the greatest hitting record of all. Recall also that the next year was an expansion season, when baseball added eight games to the schedule, when Roger Maris broke Ruth's single-season record, and home runs rose from 136 per team to 153 per team. Would 14 home runs have been unreasonable? Not at all.

Of course, all that is idle speculation, mere barroom talk. Even if Williams had somehow broken Ruth's record, it doesn't seem likely that he could have hit enough to hold off Hank Aaron barely a decade later.

Besides, Ted would be the first to tell you that millions of other guys sacrificed much more during those wars.

WHICH CELTICS PLAYER HAD THE MOST UNIQUE CAREER AFTER HANGIN' 'EM UP?

Even had he not gone on to greater fame as television's *The Rifleman*, Kevin "Chuck" Connors still would have been remembered for the one full season he played with the Boston Celtics.

On November 5, 1946, the night the Celtics played their first home game in the newly formed Basketball Association of America, tipoff had to be delayed for more than an hour when Connors, a 25-year-old Brooklyn native who came to Boston by way of Seton Hall University, destroyed a wooden backboard while making a dunk during warm-ups. Workers from the Boston Garden had to send a truck across town to the Boston Arena to fetch a spare backboard, after which the Celtics dropped a 57-55 decision to the Chicago Stags.

153

Connors, athletic-looking, 6'7", and weighing 205 pounds, appeared in 49 of the Celtics' 50 games during the '46-47 season, averaging 4.6 points. He appeared in just four games the following season, and then set off to pursue another calling: baseball.

Signed by his hometown Brooklyn Dodgers, he appeared in one big-league game with the Bums in 1949, and then was traded to the Chicago Cubs. He played in 66 games for the Cubs in 1951, hitting .239 with two home runs in 201 at-bats, including a ninth-inning shot off Giants great Sal Maglie. According to lore, the lanky first baseman earned his nickname because of the way he "chucked" the ball back to the pitcher after infield practice. Remember, this is the man who broke the backboard in the Celtics' first home game.

When the Cubs sent Connors to the minor leagues, it was the break of a lifetime. Playing for the Los Angeles Angels in the Pacific Coast League, "... he hit a home run, and then did cartwheels as he ran around the bases," says Jeff Connors, one of the actor/athlete's four sons. "It just so happened that there was a talent scout at the ballpark that day, and I guess you could say my dad was discovered."

Connors landed a small part in *Pat and Mike*, directed by the great George Cukor and starring two Hollywood heavyweights: Spencer Tracy and Katharine Hepburn. He did bit parts in other movies and television programs, including a 1954 episode of *The Adventures of Superman*, in which he played a mule-riding fellow named Sylvester J. Superman, who gets confused for the real Superman, and, well, hilarity ensues.

Connors' big break came in 1958, when he was cast as Lucas McCain in *The Rifleman*, a television western about a rifle-toting rancher and single parent who teaches valuable life lessons to his son, played by Johnny Crawford, while keeping the town of North Fork free of bad guys. The show ran until 1963. Connors later starred in the television series *Branded*, a short-lived program perhaps better known for its opening sequence, in which Connors' Jason McCord character suffers the humiliation of being drummed out of the army for cowardice. (He's no coward, of course, as he proves in each episode.)

That Chuck Connors was always an athlete at heart was clear. "He was very, very proud that he played for the Boston Celtics and then played big-league baseball," says Jeff Connors, a musician and onetime actor who as a child landed a role in a Rifleman episode.

Chuck Connors died of cancer in 1992 and is buried at San Fernando Mission Cemetery in Mission Hills, California. His grave marker contains a photograph of him as Lucas McCain, holding his Winchester rifle. Revealingly, the marker also contains the logos of the Brooklyn Dodgers, Chicago Cubs . . . and Boston Celtics.

WHICH BRUINS PLAYER HAD THE MOST UNIQUE CAREER AFTER HANGIN' 'EM UP?

58 Lyndon Byers was a self-professed goon who carved out parts of 10 seasons in the National Hockey League, mostly with the Boston Bruins. But by September 1995 he had long since become a minor-league vagabond, trying one last time to make it back to the NHL—this time with the Hartford Whalers—after having kicked around for years with such outfits as the Kansas City Blades and Las Vegas Thunder.

"The Whalers were going to send me back to the minors, to Springfield, and I asked myself, 'Do I really need this?'" Byers recalled. "I would have been in the American Hockey League, getting in fights with these 6'5" 19-year-old kids who'd have loved to knock me on my ass to show how tough they are."

His career over at the age of 31, Byers returned home to British Columbia to help his parents run the bar he had purchased for them. That lasted about two weeks. Byers eventually drifted back to Boston, where he picked up some work talking hockey on a Sunday night television program. This led to more work in media, and he became a part-time yakker on WEEI, Boston's dominant sports talk-radio station. Proving to be as freewheeling and unpredictable over the airwaves as he had been on the ice, Byers landed a full-time gig as sports director and morning gabber at WAAF, a hardcore rock station.

The transition wasn't always easy. A second conviction for driving under the influence resulted in a 60-day jail sentence, which Byers served. Upon his release, Byers spoke to youth groups about the evils of drinking and driving, and then resumed his radio career.

During his hockey days, Byers had struck up a friendship with the actor Michael J. Fox, a fellow Canadian and a lifelong hockey enthusiast. In 2003, Fox wrote a pilot for a television series, *Hench at Home*, a comedy about the travails of a recently retired hockey player. Byers was asked to audition for the lead role.

"I flew to New York for this thing, not having an idea in the world what an audition was all about," he said. "I'm standing in front of this camera, not knowing what to do, so I spent 10 minutes telling this woman about the time a bear chased my grandfather around a trailer in Saskatchewan.

"I knew this was a big deal for Michael. It was a $3 million-dollar project, and he didn't have time to coddle me. So I did my thing and got on a plane and went back to Boston, thinking that was the end of it."

The next day, Byers was told he had landed the part. The pilot was filmed, but not picked up.

Yet acting offers continued to come his way. He has a recurring role in the television series *Rescue Me*, and he has had small roles in a number of films, including *Stuck on You*, directed by Bobby and Peter Farrelly.

"I'd love to make acting a career, but it's not as easy as picking up the phone and calling the Farrelly brothers for a job," said Byers. "It's big business, and you have to audition. I'll continue with the acting, but my career is radio now.

"I'm the biggest yap-off, wise-off on the planet, and it's the perfect place for me. Not to get all sappy or anything, but I love radio as much as I loved playing for the Bruins."

WHICH RED SOX PLAYER HAD THE MOST UNIQUE CAREER AFTER HANGIN' 'EM UP?

Carmen Fanzone kicked around the minors for seven years before he finally made it to the big leagues, pinch hitting for Jim Lonborg in the eighth inning of a July 21, 1970, game at Fenway Park.

The next day, he started at third base and made two errors on the same play.

"What I remember most," he would say years later, "is hearing, 'Error, Fanzone. Error Fanzone.' It was two errors, so they said my name twice. I was really demoralized, really down. After the game, hardly anybody in the clubhouse said anything to me. (Carl) Yastrzemski was on the team, and he was supposed to be a leader, but he didn't say a word. I was feeling so bad about myself that it would have been nice to hear a good word from somebody."

Fanzone played just 10 games for the Red Sox that year, getting three hits in 15 at-bats. During the off season he was traded to the Chicago Cubs for another utility player, Phil Gagliano.

But it was after baseball—including parts of four seasons with the Cubs, for whom he hit a home run in his first at-bat, along with the requisite back-and-forth trips to the minors—that he found his life's calling. He had grown up in what he likes to call "a musical family" and had taken to the trumpet, eventually earning a degree in music at Central Michigan University.

Turning full time to music after his baseball career ended, he landed a gig playing trumpet for the Baja Marimba Band in New Orleans. He played with the Jimmy Dorsey Orchestra. He backed up Tony Bennett at a show in Vancouver, Washington, and went on the road with Lou Rawls.

Somewhere along the line, a Carmen Fanzone myth emerged: That he settled in as a trumpet player on *The Tonight Show* during the Johnny Carson era.

"I wish I could say that was true, because that would be like a baseball player making the big leagues, but it never happened," said Fanzone. "I have a lot of newspaper clippings that mention I was with the *The Tonight Show*, and I don't know where it started. It's just one of those things."

Carmen Fanzone has remained active both in baseball and music over the years. He has participated in a number of Chicago Cubs "fantasy camps" (he has nicer things to say about his Cubs years than his time with the Red Sox), and he does work for the American Federation of Musicians out of Local 47 in Hollywood.

Though Fanzone was the winner in this category, much thought was given to naming Moe Berg as the Red Sox player who had the most interesting career after he hung 'em up. Berg, a journeyman catcher who was with the Red Sox from 1935 through 1939, was a Princeton man who studied as many as seven languages and is considered by many to be one of the most intelligent men ever to play the game.

Berg was also a spy, doing some of his best work during a 1934 baseball barnstorming tour of Japan. He brought along a motion-picture camera, with which he was able to shoot military installations and the like. Berg was doing his spying while still active as a baseball player, though, so he was not included in this category.

And in case you're wondering, no, Moe Berg did not play trumpet on *The Tonight Show*.

WHICH PATRIOTS PLAYER HAD THE MOST UNIQUE CAREER AFTER HANGIN' 'EM UP?

Johnny Outlaw was a 10th-round pick by the Patriots in the 1968 draft. A defensive back out of Jackson State with a cool name and fast feet, he played four seasons with the Pats, followed by seven seasons with the Philadelphia Eagles.

After his playing career ended, Outlaw eventually went into coaching. But as if to prove his athleticism wasn't limited to football, he went into basketball coaching. He has worked as an assistant to Bernie Bickerstaff with the Denver Broncos, Washington Wizards and, as of 2006, the Charlotte Bobcats.

Outlaw isn't the only former Patriot who has forged a sports career outside of football. Charlie Baumann, a place-kicker who played for the Patriots in 1991 and '92, found the business side of baseball to his liking: He's the president and co-owner of the Brevard County Manatees, a farm team for the Milwaukee Brewers in the Single-A Florida State League.

But while these two former Patriots have had interesting post-football careers, our pick as the Patriot who has had the most interesting life after Foxboro is Bill Lenkaitis, a center who played for the team from 1971 to 1981.

Lenkaitis is a dentist—which, admittedly, doesn't jump off the page as a particularly interesting profession. Even in the athletic community, jocks-turned-dentists are common. Jim Lonborg, who won the American League Cy Young Award for the pennant-winning 1967 Red Sox, is a dentist.

What sets Lenkaitis apart is the sheer size of the man: At 6'4", 260 pounds, he is one giant of a dentist. Can a man that size even get his hands inside a patient's mouth?

"Yes," said Lenkaitis, "but that doesn't stop some people from worrying, or from making the typical dumb-jock jokes. I have had a couple of old ladies who told me they weren't going to let a big football player work on their teeth."

While Lenkaitis' hands are big, he insists he's met bigger athletes with bigger hands.

Lenkaitis says that Dick Radatz, the late Red Sox relief pitcher, "had the biggest hands I have ever seen. His ring size was 18. And Jim Loscutoff, who played for the Celtics, was a 17. I'm an 11 1/2. I'm a big guy, but my hands aren't as big as people think."

Lenkaitis, who played his college football at Penn State, studied dentistry during his Patriots days, taking courses at the University of Tennessee. But even in dental school the stereotypes continued, with classmates making jokes about what they called "the jock curve."

"They'd say I was getting good grades because I'd talk football with the instructors," he said. "But my hands are as good as anybody's."

Lenkaitis' practice is located near Gillette Stadium, home of the Patriots. And his patients include some of his former Pats teammates.

"You'd be amazed," he said. "I have these big, tough ex-football players coming to see me, and some of them want to be put to sleep for a cleaning."

Charlie Baumann, the football player-turned-baseball-team-owner, admits that Leinkaitis has had the more interesting career.

"I just picture a guy that size saying, 'This won't hurt a bit,'" Baumann said. "Who'd believe him?"

WHAT WAS THE GREATEST FOOTBALL PLAY IN BOSTON HISTORY?

61 You're thinking of one of those many Vinatieri field goals, aren't you? Or the Brady-to-Brown touchdown in overtime. Or maybe the end of the Snow Plow game. Well, you're wrong. Oh, those were great plays all right, and we would have loved to hear John Madden explain the Snow Plow field goal with his telestrator. "And then the prison release worker drives the snowplow onto the field and, doink, clears a space for Smith to kick the game-winning field goal—boom!" But you've got the wrong Boston team. For sheer "Set-the-Defibrillator-Dial-to-11" drama, nothing beats Doug Flutie's Hail Mary pass when Boston College beat Miami in 1984.

Today, when college football is literally played five days a week and broadcast from nearly sunup to midnight each Saturday, it's important to remember that it wasn't like that in 1984. Back then there still were just a handful of games shown each week, and those few were special. This was especially true of that year's Boston College—Miami game. Miami was the reigning national champion, while Boston College was the lovable underdog led by the Flutie, the little quarterback who set the NCAA records for yards passing and goosebumps raised.

The game was played on the day after Thanksgiving in a rainstorm. Flutie and Miami quarterback Bernie Kosar combined for more than 900 yards, 84 passes, 59 completions, five touchdowns, and enough highlights to fill a week on ESPN Classic. The lead changed hands four times in the fourth quarter alone, with the final change appearing to come when Miami scored a touchdown with 28 seconds left to take a 45-41 lead.

But with Flutie as quarterback, 28 seconds were practically as long as a PBS pledge drive. As long as he had the ball in his hands there was always hope. Sure enough, Flutie completed two quick passes to get BC to the 48-yard-line with six seconds left. There was time for one last play. Flutie took the snap, scrambled as if trapped in a Frogger arcade game, found himself back at the BC 40, then hurled the ball as far as his arm and heart could manage. The pass sailed over three Miami defenders and into the arms of wide receiver Gerard Phelan in the endzone for the game-winning touchdown.

Officially, that Hail Mary was a 48-yard touchdown pass. Unofficially, it not only is the greatest single play in Boston football history, it's the greatest play in college football history that doesn't involve a tuba and the Stanford band.

WHO WAS THE WORST COACH IN PATRIOTS HISTORY?

Rod Rust was always highly respected for his ability to run a National Football League defense. Consider, for example, what took place midway through the 1984 season, when then-Patriots coach Ron Meyer sacked Rust as his defensive coordinator. Team owner Billy Sullivan stepped in and fired Meyer, brought in Raymond Berry to be his new head coach

. . . and promptly re-hired Rust as defensive coordinator.

But not all assistant coaches—in any sport—are cut out to be the head man, the walking boss. And so it was with Rust, who would replace Berry as head coach in 1990 and guide the team to its worst record—1-15—in franchise history.

It's true that Rust wasn't working with players on the verge of morphing into a football powerhouse. But after winning their second game of the season, 16-14 over the Indianapolis Colts, the Pats stumbled through the rest of the schedule, losing 14 consecutive games. In only three of those games were the Patriots within seven points of their opponent at the final whistle.

Along the way there was off-field chaos. When *Boston Herald* sportswriter Lisa Olson accused some Patriots players of exposing themselves in her presence, the fall-out from the controversy haunted the team for the remainder of the season. While Rust cannot be blamed for the Olson incident, a picture nonetheless emerges of a team without leadership, without discipline.

The low point of this going-nowhere season was a November 12 game against the Colts at Foxboro Stadium. The Pats came into the game at 1-7, the Colts 2-6—not exactly a playoff preview. When it was over, with the Colts emerging with a sloppy, haphazard 13-10 victory over the Patriots before a gathering of 28,924, Rust walked into a weight room that in those days was used as a postgame interview room and said, "I'm proud of my players . . . I'm proud of 'em. I'm sorry they didn't play well enough to win, but it's clear our intensity level was excellent."

This is not what Patriots fans wanted to hear. The team's next two home games attracted crowds of 26,280 and 22,286, which, not counting games with replacement players in 1987, was the lowest attendance for a Pats home game since 1969, the last year of the American Football League, when the team was playing at Boston College's Alumni Stadium.

Rust was relieved of his duties—and, probably, relieved himself—at the end of the season. He returned to his previous life as a defensive coordinator.

On February 13, 2006, the Ottawa Renegades of the Canadian Football League named Rust as their defensive coordinator for the upcoming season. In making the announcement, the Renegades posted this quote from head coach John Jenkins on their web site: "Rod Rust . . . is an excellent teacher of pro football defensive schemes and he will indeed elevate the performance of these Ottawa Renegade defensive players."

A little wordy, but nonetheless an affirmation of Rust's ability to run a football defense. It was running the entire operation that was the problem.

DUMB AND DUMBER: WHAT WAS THE WORST MOVE BY A RED SOX MANAGER?

Sheesh. And Meryl Streep thought she had a tough decision to make in *Sophie's Choice*. Let's get right to the nominees . . .

JOE MCCARTHY STARTS DENNY GALEHOUSE, 1948

In the first playoff game in American League history, Boston manager Joe McCarthy infamously chose to start Denny Galehouse against Cleveland because he didn't want to start Mel Parnell on three days' rest. Plus Galehouse was well rested and experienced in big games. Galehouse, of course, gave up four runs and didn't get out of the fourth that day. Should McCarthy have started Mel Parnell (15-8, 3.14 ERA) or Ellis Kinder (who gave up four runs in relief) instead? Sure, but we also should have drained our bank accounts, taken out a second mortgage, flown to Vegas, and put every cent we owned down on the Red Sox to win the 2004 World Series just as soon as they fell behind the Yankees 3-0 in the ALCS. Galehouse has gone down in history as a terrible choice, but he wasn't a bad pitcher. He was 8-7 heading into the playoff game, with 109 career wins. Unfortunately, he never would win a 110th game, pitching only two innings after 1948 and going down in Boston infamy.

Choosing Galehouse wasn't a ridiculously stupid choice, just a bad one.

DON ZIMMER BLOWS OUT THE 1978 RED SOX

The Sox led the league by 10 games in July and the Yankees by 14½ but we all know what happened after that. The Gerbil stuck with his regulars to the extent that everyone (other than Jim Rice) was worn out by September. All the bench players combined had just 645 at-bats the entire season, or fewer at-bats than Rice had by himself. No other manager in the league so seldom used his bench. In Zimmer's defense, though, it's not like anyone on the bench was anyone you really wanted in your lineup.

JOHN MCNAMARA FAILS TO SUB FOR BILL BUCKNER, 1986

Manager John McNamara's real mistake in Game 6 was not leaving Buckner at first base in the tenth inning; it was not getting him out of the game several innings earlier. McNamara should have pinch hit Don Baylor for Buckner in the eighth inning when the Red Sox led 3-2 with runners on first and second and lefty Jesse Orosco on the mound. Instead, he left Buckner in the game to bat—he flied out—

and he was still on the field two innings later when Mookie Wilson hit that dribbler to first base. He also should have used Oil Can Boyd in relief to preserve the lead in Game 7 when Bruce Hurst tired.

GRADY LITTLE STAYS TOO LONG WITH PEDRO

Years later, you can still hear the curses echoing throughout Boston. How could Grady have been so stubborn? How could he have been so stupid? Yeah, Pedro was his ace, but everyone knew he was tiring. The evidence was clear that Pedro's effectiveness declined significantly once he got past 100 pitches. And he was past that mark when he faced Derek Jeter with one out and no one on base. He gave up a double to Jeter on pitch 110 . . . and Grady stayed with him. He gave up a run-scoring single on pitch 115 . . . and Grady stayed with him. He gave up a run-scoring double to Hideki Matsui on pitch 118 . . . and Grady stayed with him. Finally, after Pedro gave up a game-tying single on pitch 123, Grady finally went to the bullpen.

Yeah, McNamara made a big mistake when he left Buckner out there. But a limping first baseman normally can only do so much damage. A tiring starting pitcher? That's much different. All focus was on Pedro. Everyone in the stadium, and everyone watching on TV, knew he had to come out. Grady, though, watched him give up hit after hit after hit until it was too late.

"I wouldn't put Grady on the spot like that whatsoever,"

Pedro said after the game. "I am the ace of the team. I wasn't thinking about pitch counts then. That is no time to say I'm tired. There is no reason to blame Grady. He doesn't play the game. We do. I do. If you want to blame someone, blame me. I walk out there. I'm responsible for the pitches I make in the middle of the game."

That's true, but Grady was responsible for leaving him out there too long. The most important thing a manager can do is put his players in a position to succeed. Instead, Grady left Pedro in a position to fail. Great pitchers are too competitive to say they're tired and need to come out in such a situation. The manager must make that decision for them.

Of the Red Sox managers who made painful, horrible mistakes, Grady is the only one who immediately paid for it with his job. And he should have. Grady made some very strange pitching moves in the Division Series that fall—he used two starters in Game 1—and got away with them. He didn't get away with this one.

(Oh, and while we're at it—what's with all those people who reacted to the 2004 World Series by saying they now forgive Buckner? Forgive Buckner? What, are they going to follow that up by "forgiving" Tony C. for not getting out of the way and Darryl Stingley for dropping the ball? He made an error, people. An untimely, unfortunate, unforgettable error, but an error all the same. If we start condemning players to eternal damnation for making errors, Manny Ramirez better layer on some extra sunscreen.)

171

WHO WAS THE WORST MANAGER IN RED SOX HISTORY?

64 Though he had his detractors, Joe Kerrigan was a highly regarded pitching coach when he joined the Red Sox for the 1997 season. Such was general manager Dan Duquette's determination to bring Kerrigan to Boston that he took the unusual step of making the hire even before he had recruited a new manager, Kevin Kennedy having been let go the day after the '96 season ended.

The new manager would be Jimy Williams, who remained in place for nearly five seasons, until his ever-souring relationship with Duquette finally—some would say mercifully—cost him his job with six weeks remaining in the 2001 season.

But while Kerrigan and Duquette had remained close, it was nonetheless a shocking development when, on the afternoon of August 16, 2001, Kerrigan appeared in a conference room to meet the media in his new role as manager of the Boston Red Sox.

Though he had never managed at any level of baseball, Kerrigan was given not just the interim managerial keys to the Red Sox, but also a deal that extended through the

2002 season. Hey, when you're that good of a pitching coach, you don't settle for some interim babysitting job.

But the clubhouse he inherited was not merely dysfunctional, but fixing for a rebellion. The players were well aware that Williams had had his legs cut out from under him by Duquette, and now they were expected to answer to a rookie skipper who was the general manager's pet—some would say his puppet.

And it was a disaster. Kerrigan had promised, in his introductory press conference, that Red Sox fans would be seeing a set lineup—a direct repudiation of Williams's daily tinkering with the lineup. But the new manager was the same as the old manager: a new lineup every day.

Players openly rebelled. There were episodes on charter flights, in the clubhouse, on the practice field. He pitched a clearly ailing Pedro Martinez in a game against the Yankees, with the right-hander lasting just three innings. After the game, the manager barked at sportswriters who questioned the move, asking one of them, "What do you know about arm slots?"

On the day Kerrigan became manager, the Red Sox were 65-53 in the American League East, five games behind the Yankees. The Sox won Kerrigan's debut, topping the Seattle Mariners, and went on to win six of the new manager's first nine games.

And then the Red Sox lost nine straight games, dropping them to 9½ games behind the Yankees. The season was

173

fading away under Kerrigan's watch. After ending the nine-game streak, the Sox went out and lost another four in a row.

Though the Red Sox would win the final five games of this dismal season, the Kerrigan log was not pretty. The Sox went 17-26, finishing 13½ games behind the Yankees.

Duquette was determined to bring Kerrigan back as manager for the 2002 season. There was one small problem: The Red Sox were sold during the off season, and the new ownership group, headed up by John W. Henry, had a different plan.

Among their first moves: Duquette and Kerrigan were fired.

Joe Kerrigan's tenure as manager of the Red Sox lasted just 43 games.

SHOULD TEAMS PROMOTE A PITCHING COACH TO MANAGER?

While we're on the subject, when the time comes to replace Terry Francona as manager (and it will happen, either through dismissal or retirement), the Red Sox should not replace him with Al Nipper or Dave Wallace or whoever their pitching coach is at the time. Not because we think Wallace and

Nipper are bad pitching coaches; to the contrary, we're believe they are good pitching coaches, very good.

And the better they are, the more reason there is to keep them as pitching coaches and out of the manager's seat. A good pitching coach can be much more valuable than a manager by significantly improving the staff. A pitching coach who turns a 10-game winner into a 20-game winner has a much more dramatic impact on a team, even though he never fills out a single lineup card or kicks dirt on a single umpire.

Is this hiring policy unfair to pitching coaches who aspire to higher positions? Absolutely. But who said baseball is fair? Certainly not Red Sox fans.

Three things can happen when you promote a pitching coach to manager. Two of them are bad. One, you lose a proven pitching coach. Two, you gain a weak manager. Three, you gain a good manager—though this is hardly worth risking outcomes one or two when there are other good candidates.

The Red Sox learned this lesson with Kerrigan, but they aren't the only team to have done so. Ray Miller was considered one of the game's best pitching coaches when he was the Baltimore Orioles pitching coach in the late 70s and early 80s. The Twins hired him away as manager in 1985, but fired him less than two years later when he flopped in the job. He caught on with Pittsburgh as the Pirates pitching coach, where he again worked his magic.

The Orioles re-hired him as pitching coach in the early 90s and he continued his success. Then the Orioles made the classic blunder of elevating him to manager in 1998—with predictable results. A team that went wire to wire the previous year finished below .500 and still hasn't recovered. The Orioles fired Miller after two seasons.

Which is not to say that pitching coaches can't be good managers—Roger Craig, who developed the split-fingered fastball, guided the Giants to two division titles and their first pennant in a generation. It also doesn't mean that teams shouldn't hire another team's pitching coach to be manager. Hiring away someone's else coach changes the equation dramatically. Of the three possible outcomes, two of them are good. One, you may be hiring a bad manager, but that's always a risk. Two, you may be hiring a good manager. Three, you are weakening a rival by taking away its most valuable coach.

Which is why the Red Sox should hire the Yankees pitching coach whenever possible.

WHO WAS REALLY AT FAULT IN THE ED ARMBRISTER PLAY?

66 You know the situation. Game 3 of the 1975 World Series, bottom of the tenth, score tied 5-5, Cincinnati's Cesar Geronimo on first base. Ed Armbrister lays down a bunt that barely gets past home plate. He and catcher Carlton Fisk have a brief encounter. Pudge tosses the ball into center field. Umpire Larry Barnett sees nothing wrong, leaving Armbrister at first and Geronimo on third. Joe Morgan singles home Geronimo. Reds win and take 2-1 lead in the series.

Now, had there been 24-hour sports talk in 1975, there would have been so many angry calls the next day that Kevin from Somerville still would be on hold. As it was, NBC broadcasters Tony Kubek and Curt Gowdy criticized Barnett's call so much that the umpire said he subsequently received death threats from hysterical Boston fans.

But who really was most at fault? Barnett? Armbrister? Or Fisk?

Armbrister laid down a very bad bunt that went only a bit past home plate. Fielding the ball, Fisk got entangled with Armbrister on his way to first. Under most circumstances, if

177

a baserunner interferes with a fielder for any reason—whether the contact is accidental or intentional—the runner is out. Armbrister did not get out of the way, so he should have been called out and Geronimo sent back to first.

At least, that was the reasoning behind the NBC broadcasters' criticism of Barnett. However, according to a footnote in Roger Angell's account of the series in *Five Seasons*, Major League Baseball revealed after the World Series what amounted to a little-known codicil in the Faber Constitution—err, in the rules—that exempts a baserunner of interference in just such a situation. This codicil is now officially included in the rule book as a comment to 7.09(j): "When a catcher and batter-runner going to first base have contact when the catcher is fielding the ball, there is generally no violation and nothing should be called."

That rule seemingly exonerates both Armbrister and Barnett, though, as Angell points out, it would have been nice had baseball defended its beleaguered umpire by explaining the codicil at the time of the play rather than waiting several weeks—by which time everyone's mind was made up, and Barnett had to change his phone number, grow a beard, and walk around in dark glasses.

So who was most to blame? Well, blame is too harsh a word but Fisk certainly could have saved everyone a lot of time and anguish by simply tagging Armbrister when the two bumped, then calmly throwing to second base for the double play on Geronimo. Instead, he rushed his throw, made the worst of the situation, and sparked a World Series controversy that still prompts arguments near closing time.

Sigh. It was a bad blow, but at least Tim McCarver was an active player back then. If he were in the broadcast booth that night, he would have reviewed and overanalyzed the play so much that the World Series would have run into November.

THE BOSTON ATHLETE YOU NEVER GOT USED TO SEEING IN ANOTHER UNIFORM

67 During the 1969-70 NBA season, seven years after he had ended his brilliant playing career with the Celtics, Bob Cousy returned to the hardwood via a seven-game stint with the Cincinnati Royals.

In 1991, after 19 seasons manning right field for the Red Sox, Dwight Evans logged one last season with the Baltimore Orioles.

Drew Bledsoe returned to Foxboro as a member of the Buffalo Bills. Dave Cowens became a Milwaukee Buck, Johnny Damon a Yankee. William Weld, after twice being elected governor of Massachusetts, flirted with a run for governor of New York.

And then there's the flip side: Babe Ruth stumbling through the last days of his career in a Boston Braves uniform.

But no public figure in Boston history ever looked more out of place than Bobby Orr during the parts of two seasons he played with the Chicago BlackHawks. To Bruins fans of the 1970s, it was like seeing Archie Bunker showing up at a peace rally, or the Doors playing backup to Kate Smith.

Such were the sizzling scouting reports from the Canadian junior hockey ranks that Orr was already a celebrity when he arrived in Boston in 1966. Almost overnight he became a Boston sports icon. He led the Bruins to Stanley Cup championships in 1970 and 1972, with the understanding that the decade would produce many more championship seasons. The best example of Orr's cultlike following in Boston is that the Bruins of that era were known as "Bobby Orr and the Big, Bad Bruins."

Yet there he was in 1976, skating with his new team, the Chicago BlackHawks. Orr had been steered to the Midwest by his agent, Alan Eagleson, who told the hockey superstar that the BlackHawks had come up with a better offer than the Bruins'. One small problem: It wasn't true.

Not only had the Bruins put a lucrative deal on the table, they also offered Orr an ownership stake in the team. It turns out Eagleson, by now the executive director of the National Hockey League Players Association in addition to serving as an agent for a stable of clients, was a scam artist.

Thanks to the reporting of Russ Conway of the *Eagle Tribune* of Lawrence, Massachusetts and the dogged determination of several ex-NHL players, notably Orr, Eagleson eventually served prison time for mail fraud and embezzlement. But the truth wouldn't be known for many years, long after Orr's career had ended. By the time this all came to light, Orr was wearing neither a Bruins nor a BlackHawks uniform; he was now wearing a suit, a Boston businessman working out of a Back Bay office.

The BlackHawks had had big plans for Orr. "Chicago hoping for gold with Orr," proclaimed the headline in *The Hockey News*. But Orr's knees were shot, and his brilliant career ended too soon. He played in only 20 games for the BlackHawks in 1976-77, with four goals and 19 assists. The following season, his last in the NHL, he played in just six games, with two goals and two assists.

Yet the pictures remain, and, to Bruins fans, they are frightening: Bobby Orr, No. 4, carrying the puck up ice in a BlackHawks uniform.

To the true Bruins fan, time has not healed this wound.

WHICH WAS THE GREATER FEAT: DIMAGGIO'S HITTING STREAK OR BATTING .406?

68 More than six decades after the fact, with both players dead and gone, the debate goes on: Which was the greater accomplishment in 1941, Joe DiMaggio hitting safely in a record 56 consecutive games (breaking the previous record by a dozen games) or Ted Williams batting. 406 (the last person to do so)?

Most fans then and now pick DiMaggio. And most fans are wrong.

We know, we know. Eight players have hit .400 in modern history, including five who hit better than Ted's .406, while three have come within striking distance of that mark in the past three decades—Tony Gwynn's .394 average in 1994, George Brett's .390 in 1980, and Rod Carew's .388 in 1977. Meanwhile, no one else in major league history has ever come within 12 games of DiMaggio's record.

How difficult was DiMaggio's streak? Pete Rose has come closest to matching it, but even after hitting in 44 consecutive games in 1978, he still finished two weeks short of breaking the record. Statisticians calculate that a

56-game hitting streak should occur anywhere from once every thousand years to once every 18,000 years. Or about the same odds as Keanu Reeves winning an Oscar.

But what do those numbers really prove? If those odds were truly accurate, then DiMaggio would never have hit in 56 games. But he did, so it's reasonable to assume that maybe those calculations are about as accurate as ours are when we balance our checkbooks at the end of the month.

Besides, it's not about the odds. We're not asking which feat is less likely. Getting hit by lightning is less likely than raising a child to be an intelligent, caring adult, but which is the greater accomplishment? Look at it this way: DiMaggio batted .408 with 15 home runs, 55 RBIs, and 56 runs during his hitting streak. During that same span, Ted batted .413 with 12 home runs, 49 RBIs, and 54 runs in 53 games. DiMaggio's streak may have drawn more attention, but Ted had just as good a run. And when you include walk totals, he had a more productive run.

A long hitting streak is impressive, but is always due to a certain amount of luck—a seeing-eye single, a tough hop, a third baseman shading the line or a kindly scorer. But to hit .400? There is no luck involved. It requires a level of skill and consistency over an entire season, not just two months.

While DiMaggio maintained his streak despite the pressure of national attention, it's not as if Ted had it easy, either. True, he could go hitless here and there without ending his quest. But he endured considerable pressure as

183

well. In fact, he not only endured the pressure, he brought more upon himself. With a .3995 batting average that would have rounded up to .400, Ted not only played the final day of the season, he played both ends of a double-header. And in what remains one of the greatest perform-ances under pressure in baseball history, Ted went 6-for-8 to lift his average to .406 . . . and complete the greatest bat-ting feat of 1941.

WHO WAS BETTER, TED OR DIMAGGIO?

There were three types of people in the United States in the 1940s. Those who believed that Ted Williams was the greatest player in base-ball, those who believed that Joe DiMaggio was the greatest player in baseball, and those who didn't know what the @#&$ they were talking about.

The Ted or Joe debate flared especially hot in 1941. DiMaggio hit in 56 consecutive games and won the MVP. Williams hit .406 and finished second. Who was more valu-able? DiMaggio hit .357 with 30 home runs, 122 runs, 125 RBIs, 76 walks, a .440 on-base percentage, and a 1.083 OPS. Great numbers, right? Well, in addition to batting .406, Williams hit 37 home runs with 120 RBIs, 135 runs, 147 walks, a .553 on-base percentage, and a 1.287 OPS. Ted's numbers not only were significantly better than DiMaggio's, they were so extraordinary that if he had posted them today, he would be asked to pee in a bottle and testify before Congress.

So Ted deserved the MVP that year? Not so fast. DiMaggio also was one of the greatest fielders in baseball history. Ted? Not so much. Legend has it that he stood in the outfield taking imaginary swings of the bat when he was in the minors. Manny Ramirez looks like Ichiro by comparison.

Ted's attitude toward fielding can be summed up best by this memory of Twins bullpen coach Rick Stelmaszek, who played for Williams when Ted managed the Senators. The team was going over fundamental drills in spring training when coaches Joe Camacho and Nellie Fox got into an argument over how to execute a rundown.

"They get into a heated argument. I mean heated," Stelmaszek recalled. "I thought it was going to come to blows. They're arguing like two little kids. And you've got all the pitchers, the infielders, the catchers standing around watching them. So here comes Big Ted.

"'WHAT'S UP? WHAT'S UP?'

"'He wants to run it that way.'

"'He wants to run it that way.'

"'Screw that, Eddie Stanky told me to do it this way.'

"So, Big Ted takes a look at the two of them, sizes up the situation and says, 'F*&%@ it! LET'S HIT!' And we never

185

had another fundamental drill that spring."

Joe also was the superior baserunner, though because it was a different era he almost never took advantage of that skill, stealing just 30 bases his entire career. There's no point counting World Series rings because we all know how lopsided those numbers are, and besides, they don't measure how good a player was nearly as much as they measure how good his teammates were.

So the argument comes down to this. As a hitter, Ted's 162-game average was .344 with 37 home runs, 130 RBIs, 127 runs, 143 walks, a .482 on-base percentage, and a 1.116 OPS. Joe's was .325, 34 HRs, 143 RBIs, 130 runs, 74 walks, .398 on-base percentage, and a .977 OPS. Ted has a significant edge in average, walks, OBP, and OPS, but the production numbers are a wash. Defensively, however, there was just no comparison between the two.

If we were drafting for our fantasy team, we'd pick Ted in a heartbeat. But in the real game fielding counts, and if you were the general manager of a real team you would have to pick the guy who was a great fielder and a great hitter over the guy who was just a great hitter. And that was the Yankee.

We know, we know, you're not convinced. Just don't bother emailing us—our mailboxes are already full with hate mail from other outraged Boston fans.

SO SHOULD THE RED SOX HAVE TRADED TED WILLIAMS FOR JOE DIMAGGIO?

70 Legend has it that one night before the 1947 season Red Sox owner Tom Yawkey got drunk and agreed to trade Ted Williams to the Yankees for Joe DiMaggio. When he woke up sober the next day he thought better of the idea and called off the trade. Ever since then, fans have argued over how such a trade would have changed the fortunes of both teams.

DiMaggio, after all, hit right handed, yet played half his games at Yankee Stadium where the power alley in left-center was a staggering 457 feet from home plate. How many more home runs would he have hit had he played half his games at Fenway Park, where the left field wall was, allegedly, 310 feet down the line? Conversely, how many more home runs would Ted have hit had he played half his games in Yankee Stadium, with its cozy right field corner less than 300 feet down the line?

Further, how would placing DiMaggio and all his World Series experience into the Red Sox lineup have affected Boston's October fate? Would they have won that one-game playoff against Cleveland in 1948? Would they have held off the Yankees the final weekend of the 1949 season? Would they have played in more than one World Series during that era? Would they have—gasp!—actually won one as well? Or would Ted have lifted the Yankees to even higher levels? With Ted battering the right-field bleachers, would New York have won every World Series from 1947-1960, instead of just most of them? Or would the trade have been a wash, benefiting each team equally?

Obviously, we'll never know what would have happened. We do know, however, that DiMaggio was the far superior fielder, which is what made the trade tempting.

On the other hand, we know something else even more important than the layout of the ballpark or DiMaggio's glove: The simple fact, usually forgotten during these discussions, that Ted was four years younger than DiMaggio. That's not only a crucial difference, it's the crucial difference. DiMaggio, for all his greatness, missed nearly an entire season worth of games from 1947-51 and was out of baseball by the next season. Ted, meanwhile, still had seven more seasons (not counting the 1952 and 1953 seasons he lost to military service), two more hitting titles, and nearly 200 more home runs left in his bat.

So did Yawkey make the right decision when he sobered up? Absolutely. The Yankees wouldn't have been interested enough to consider a DiMaggio-Williams trade before 1947 and by then it was too late to make sense for the Red Sox. Had DiMaggio been traded to Boston in 1947, the Red Sox may not have been any better the next five seasons, but the Yankees definitely would have been even better than they were for nearly a decade after that.

Worse yet, just think how many times we would have heard about the Curse of the Splinter.

BOBBY ORR'S GREATEST GOAL: NOT!

 Had it been a simple slap shot from the point, or a tip-in from the midst of a crowd in front of the net, the goal Bobby Orr scored on May 10, 1970, would by now have faded into history, the particulars just a foggy memory from another time.

But thanks to a Superman-rescues-Metropolis flight through the air by young Mr. Orr—and thanks, too, to the alert trigger finger of a photographer named Ray Lussier—Orr's goal on that steamy Sunday afternoon, which brought the Bruins their first Stanley Cup in 29 years, will be remembered forever. How could it not: To this day, thousands of misty-eyed Bruins fans still keep a photograph of that goal—that is, *the* photograph of that goal—in a place of honor in their home.

When the Bruins matched up against the St. Louis Blues that day at the old Boston Garden, it was understood that the Stanley Cup would soon be keeping house in Boston.

The Bruins held a 3-0 series lead in the best-of-seven Stanley Cup finals against the Blues, an expansion team whose roster was dotted with such aging veterans as Al Arbour, Red Berenson, Phil Goyette, and goaltenders Glenn Hall and Jacques Plante.

This game, though, was tied 3-3 at the end of regulation, forcing sudden-death overtime. It lasted all of 40 seconds. Orr fed the puck to Derek Sanderson behind the net, and then, on a routine give-and-go, Orr moved in front of the net and awaited a return pass from Sanderson. Orr didn't so much shoot the puck as redirect it, neatly, conveniently, between the pads of 38-year-old Glenn Hall.

Orr, knowing his shot was true, was just beginning to lift up his arms in celebration when Blues defenseman Noel Picard got a piece of Orr's skate with his stick. The result: Orr flies across the crease, arms outstretched, both feet in the air.

Not far from Orr sat Ray Lussier, behind the glass, his camera trained on the scene. Shooting for the *Boston Record-American* (which eventually would morph into the *Boston Herald*), Lussier was in the perfect spot at the perfect moment, and with a click of his finger he forever linked himself with Orr's goal by taking the greatest hockey picture ever.

It's all there. Orr as Superman. Picard, a look of bemusement on his face, seeming to trip up Orr. Hall, old, tired, vanquished, appearing to fall backwards into the net.

And in the background thousands of Bruins fans, lifting their arms into the air. The Cup belonged to them.

Lussier died in 1991, but his famous photo lives on. Orr has signed thousands of copies over the years, as have Picard and Hall.

"I'll run into Glenn now and then at various events," Orr said, "and he always says, 'Is that the only goal you ever scored?'"

It's a special goal, Orr says, and for the obvious reason: "It was the goal that won us a Stanley Cup. And as a kid growing up in Canada, my dream was to win the Stanley Cup. And this was it."

But Hall raises a valid point: Was it the only goal Orr ever scored?

The answer, of course, is no.

But while it may have been Orr's most memorable goal, it was not his greatest goal.

Read on.

WHAT WAS BOBBY ORR'S GREATEST GOAL (FOR REAL)?

Take away the Stanley Cup and Ray Lussier's photographic wizardry, and the goal Bobby Orr scored to bring down the St. Louis Blues on May 10, 1970, was, well, just a goal. As former

Bruins coach Harry Sinden put it years later, "As goals go, it was just a pass from behind the net. Nothing special."

But let's say a space capsule was about to be hurtled into the outer reaches of the universe in search of intelligent life, and that inside that space capsule was included a collection of DVDs depicting humankind at its best—say, Michelangelo's David, or Billie Holiday singing "The Very Thought of You," or George Costanza dragging the Yankees' World Series trophy around the Yankee Stadium parking lot. And let's say that some sporting fellow at NASA insisted that a Bobby Orr goal also be included. Working within that framework, there's just no way you'd want to send Bobby Orr converting a routine give-and-go into outer space.

Instead, you'd send them the goal Orr scored against the Atlanta Flames on November 10, 1974.

On the ice in a shorthanded situation, Orr took the puck from behind his own net and skated up the middle of the ice as far as the red line, whereupon he began drifting to the right. For some reason, every Atlanta player on the ice seemed to drift right along with him. Going to his backhand at the top of the face-off circle and moving toward the net, Orr jostled the puck a little, just enough to suggest to Flames goaltender Dan Bouchard that he was going to shoot.

Instead, Orr went behind the net. And now Bouchard, like every other Atlanta player, was out of position. Orr completed his journey around the net, and then directed a lazy backhander into the empty net.

D. Leo Monahan, covering the game for the old *Boston Herald American*, wrote the following: " . . . Bobby Orr—there's that name again—scored a super-sensational-tremendous-marvelous-boy-look-at-that!   goal, shorthanded and unassisted, at 1:24 of the second period."

Monahan advised his readers that the goal ". . . will be on Channel 38's replays all summer, so catch it again for the sheer artistry. It was, well, er, ah, it was another Bobby Orr special, and the B's fans are becoming jaded with them—they come so often."

Don Cherry, the Bruins' coach at the time, later commented on the goal in an essay he contributed to *Remembering Bobby Orr*, edited by Craig MacInnis.

"He looked back and put his stick on his knees and put his head down, because he'd embarrassed the other team," Cherry wrote.

That's exactly what the replay shows. Having skated through and around five Atlanta skaters—untouched—and having pulled the goaltender out of the net, and having backhanded the puck into an empty net, Orr is the only Bruins player who isn't celebrating.

With apologies to D. Leo Monahan, words do not do justice to the greatness of this goal. You must see it.

WHO'S HAD A BETTER CAREER, BEN AFFLECK OR LOU MERLONI?

73 OK, it doesn't bring the heat of the Williams/DiMaggio, Russell/Chamberlain, or Brady/Manning debates. But then again, Boston fans already know who they would pick in those comparisons. But Ben Affleck or Lou Merloni? That's trickier.

The debate began during the 2002 season when Affleck sat in on a Red Sox broadcast and criticized Merloni, who was batting .208 at the time. Affleck said Merloni was bad for team chemistry and cited the player's complaint about a recent demotion to the minors. "He said the Red Sox sending him down was making a mockery of his career . . . Hitting .192 is making a mockery of your career."

Naturally, Merloni took offense. "Mockery?" he responded. "A mockery is his last four movies, that's a mockery, I've seen them. . . . He's got enough issues to worry about."

Who has had the better career so far, Affleck or Merloni?

The Pride of Framingham, Merloni homered in his first at-bat at Fenway. He has played parts of nine seasons in the majors, only once getting into as many as half his team's games. The Red Sox sent him up and down between Boston and AAA Pawtucket so often that it became known as the Merloni Shuttle. The Red Sox even got rid of him twice—selling him to Japan's Yokohama Bay Stars in 1999 and losing him on waivers to the San Diego Padres in 2003—but he wound up back in Boston each time. He left the Red Sox for good after the 2003 season and has played for a different team each year since. As this book went to press, he had a .271 career batting average and 14 home runs.

Affleck, meanwhile, grew up in Cambridge with his friend, Matt Damon. He had small parts in a number of movies and TV shows before winning an Academy Award for co-writing *Good Will Hunting* with Damon. This was the Hollywood equivalent of Davey Johnson hitting 43 home runs in 1973 despite never hitting more than 18 in any of his other dozen seasons.

He went on to act in the Oscar-winning *Shakespeare in Love*, date Gwyneth Paltrow, and star in *Armageddon* and *Pearl Harbor*, both of which grossed $450 million apiece despite poor reviews. He also was picked to replace Harrison Ford in the series of Jack Ryan movies.

Unfortunately, that's when the Curse of Merloni struck. After ripping Sweet Lou on the radio, Affleck not only made a staggering string of critical and box office flops—including the infamously bad *Gigli*, *Surviving Christmas*, and *Jersey Girl*—he also got dumped by Jennifer Lopez.

On the other hand, he married Jennifer Garner. And won $356,000 in the California State Poker Championship. And earned good reviews for his performance in *Hollywoodland*.

Still, the pick here is Merloni. For one thing, he actually played the game. For another, we never had to read a headline about him while waiting in line at the checkout stand. And most importantly, Lou had nothing to do with *Gigli*.

LEN BIAS OR REGGIE LEWIS:

Which Player's Death Had a More Dramatic Effect on the Success of the Celtics?

The Celtics won their 16th—and, to date, last—NBA championship on June 8, 1986, emerging with a 114-97 victory over the Houston Rockets.

It was the Celtics' third title in six seasons, and it was accompanied by the belief that the run was going to continue.

More than merely being good, the Celtics were also smart. A 1984 trade with Seattle had landed them the second overall pick in the 1986 NBA draft, which enabled the newly crowned champions to select highly touted Maryland forward Len Bias.

Less than 48 hours later, Bias lay dead in a campus dormitory at College Park. "Cardiac arrest" was the buzz phrase of the hour, but it would later be determined that cocaine had been involved, that Bias was, at least on this occasion, a user.

At the time, nobody wanted to speak of Bias' death in basketball terms. This, after all, was a tragic circumstance. Bias was just 22 years old.

But the unfolding of history makes allowances for more critical, dispassionate analysis of fallen heroes, sports or otherwise. If modern-day historians can revisit Franklin Roosevelt's decision to launch Executive Order 9066 (the internment of Japanese Americans in relocation camps during World War II), then it's not inappropriate, 20 years later, to explore the different path the Celtics might have taken with a healthy Len Bias.

Yet the larger question that haunts Celtics fans is whether the 1993 death of Reggie Lewis, an established NBA player, had a greater bearing on history than did the death of Len Bias.

Lewis was finishing up his sixth season with the Celtics when he collapsed during an April 29, 1993 playoff game against the Charlotte Hornets. Three months later, on July 29, 1993, Lewis suffered a fatal heart attack while playing pick-up basketball at a local college.

As was the case with Bias, Lewis' death brought about rampant stories of drug abuse.

Larry Bird had already retired when Lewis died, and Kevin McHale had just finished his final season. Robert Parish would play one more season with the Celtics after Lewis died, then log a few more reduced-role campaigns with the Charlotte Hornets and Chicago Bulls.

It makes sense that the Celtics would have been a better team had Lewis lived. But it's a stretch to suggest he could have led the Celtics to another title.

Bias might have done that. He'd have been a rookie during the 1986-87 season, and a player of his skills would have saved wear and tear on Bird and McHale.

Is that, then, the answer? That Bias' death had a greater effect on the Celtics? Well, yes, but with a caveat. If the Bias loyalists are correct in saying that what happened on June 19, 1986, was a youthful indiscretion, a case can be made that he'd have had a stellar NBA career if only he'd simply gone to bed that night.

But what if, as has been whispered for years, Len Bias was a frequent cocaine abuser? Bias would then have been a time bomb, bound to go off sooner or later.

In which case, no, he was not the man who was going to help the Celtics to another championship.

WHAT WAS THE GREATEST GAME IN RED SOX HISTORY?

75 We figured we would narrow down an impossibly long list of candidates by setting a few conditions. The Red Sox must have won. The game must have been exciting on its own terms, not just because of a personal achievement or a team milestone (which eliminates the 2004 World Series sweep, in which the Sox held a lead in every single inning).

And you know what? We're still leaving out way too many deserving games. But here are our candidates:

12. May 28, 1971. If it seems like every Red Sox fan over the age of 40 claims to have been at this classic mid-season duel between Vida Blue and Sonny Siebert, maybe they were. Blue was on his way to the Cy Young, Siebert to an All-Star appearance, and so many fans sneaked/bribed their way in that people were literally sitting in the aisles for the 4-2 Sox victory. If it wasn't the largest crowd in Fenway history, it felt that way.

11. Ted Clinches 1946 Pennant. Of Ted's 521 home runs, only one didn't clear the fence. But his lone inside-the-park home run, hit against the Boudreau Shift, clinched the '46 pennant in a 1-0 victory.

10. Ernie Shore perfect in relief. For more details, see argument 13.

9. Clemens Strikes Out 20, April 29, 1986. The Rocket struck out 20 twice, but the first time, when he set the record, was the best. And thanks to Dwight Evans' three-run homer in the seventh, the Sox rallied to win the game as well. If you listen, you can still hear his fastball popping in the catcher's glove.

8. Billy Rohr's near-no-hitter. The New York home opener. Jackie Kennedy and JFK Jr. in the Yankee Stadium stands. Yaz's catch. Rohr making his major league debut and holding the Yankees hitless for 8⅔ innings before Elston Howard pokes a 2-2 pitch into right field. The 1967 "Impossible Dream" officially begins.

7. July 24, 2004, Red Sox 11, Yankees 10. The Sox were 9½ games behind the Yankees when the day began. When it ended nearly four hours, five ejections, one bench-clearing brawl, and a Bill Mueller walk-off home run later, A-Rod had replaced Derek Jeter as Public Enemy No. 1, Mariano Rivera had become vulnerable, and the 2004 world championship run was on.

6. Lonborg clinches pennant, 1967. The Red Sox played the 1967 home opener in front of just 8,234 fans. On the final day, when Lonborg beat the Twins to complete his Cy Young season, the pitcher needed police protection from the thousands of fans who swarmed the field

in the first official convention of Red Sox Nation.

5. Game 8, 1912 World Series. Yes, that's right. Game 8. Game 2 finished in a tie so they played eight that year. After pitching three games, Smoky Joe Wood pitched three innings of relief to earn the win over Christy Mathewson when Fred Snodgrass dropped a routine popup that sparked Boston's two-run rally in the bottom of the 10th to win it 3-2.

4. Smoky Joe Wood beats Walter Johnson, September 6, 1912. In addition to his three World Series victories, Smoky Joe won 34 during the regular season that year. The most famous was against Walter Johnson, when Wood had a 13-game winning streak going and the Big Train had recently won 16 in a row. With an overflow crowd watching at brand-new Fenway, Wood beat Johnson 1-0 for his 30th win. In the nearly century since, the park hasn't had a pitching duel that quite matches it.

3. Game 5, 1986 ALCS. What was it like? "If there was a bathroom on the mound," reliever Steve Crawford said of a bases-loaded situation, "I would have used it." We know the feeling. The Red Sox one strike away from winter. The police lining the field for the Angels celebration. Dave Henderson's home run. And the Sox still wouldn't win for another two innings.

2. Games 4, 5, and 6 2004 ALCS. Excuse us for placing these three games as a matched entry, but that's how

we'll always remember these games, as one long, delirious stretch of baseball, from pinch-runner Dave Roberts stealing second base by a fingernail in the ninth inning of Game 4 to those game-winning Big Papi hits in extra innings to Curt Schilling's bloody sock and A-Rod's weak slap. Sorry for the lack of more details, but we're still trying to catch our breath from it all.

And the winner is...

1. Game 6, 1975 World Series. Still the classic against which all others are judged. The three days of rain. The blown 3-0 lead. Bernie Carbo's home run. Dewey's catch. And finally, Pudge's home run. As *Boston Globe* columnist Ray Fitzgerald wrote, "Call it off. Call the seventh game off. Let the World Series stand this way, three games for the Cincinnati Reds and three for the Boston Red Sox . . . "

THE BIRD VS. PIERCE ARGUMENT

76 Let's start with a statement of the obvious: Paul Pierce is not, and never will be, a better basketball player than was Larry Bird. OK?

This is not a knock on Pierce. It's just that Bird was, well, Bird. Yet an interesting and quite accidental argument was waged during the 2005-06 season, when a couple of legends in their own right, ex-Celtics-turned-broadcasters Bob Cousy and Tommy Heinsohn, batted around the notion that, when all is said and done, Pierce might turn out to be the greatest scorer in Celtics history.

The story picked up some steam, and soon everyone had an opinion. Celtics coach Doc Rivers told the *Boston Herald's* Steve Bulpett, "I don't know who would be better. Bird was so good in every way. I would say those two you would have to put up there one and two, and the argument could go either way easy."

But Bulpett did not stop with Doc Rivers. He decided to consult another expert on this topic. He tracked down Larry Bird.

For openers, Bird responded to the question with a question. Are we talking merely about the regular season here, or are we including the playoffs?

It was Bird's way of pointing out that his seasons, more often than not, went deep into the playoffs. The Celtics won three NBA championships during the Bird era. Pierce, for all his scoring prowess (he averaged 23.5 points per game over his first eight seasons), hasn't even been to the NBA Finals.

"It's hard to compare guys that have never been to the finals to other players," Bird said. "If you gear yourself to play six months of the year, it's completely different than gearing yourself to play nine months a year. My whole focus was trying to gear myself to play nine months a year."

This argument is reminiscent of the big hullabaloo in 1988 after Oakland A's slugger Jose Canseco became the first man to hit 40 home runs and steal 40 bases in a season. Yankees legend Mickey Mantle, asked to share his thoughts on the achievement, replied, "If I had known you people would have made such a big deal out of this, I would have done it a few times myself."

In similarly legendlike demeanor, Bird told Bulpett, "You know, if I wanted to score 35 points a game—if I knew I was just going to play in the regular season—I would have been very capable of doing that. But it wasn't me. I had more talent around me than Paul had, and our whole focus was winning championships."

Bird is correct, just as the Mick was correct. Bird could have scored 35 a game. The Mick could have stolen the 40 bases. But at what cost? And to what end?

For the record, John Havlicek is the Celtics' all-time scorer with 26,395 points in 1,270 games. Bird is next with 21,791 points in 897 games. In his eight seasons, covering 605 games, Pierce has scored 14,202 points. He moved into the Celtics' top 10 during the 2005-06 season; barring injury, he was expected to pass Hall of Famers Bill Russell and Sam Jones during the 2006-07 season.

WHAT WAS THE GREATEST MOMENT IN BOSTON SPORTS HISTORY?

77 Seeing as how our clothes still stink of champagne from October 2004 and that we still can't explain how those panties got into our Houston hotel room in January 2002, it's tempting to go with the Red Sox finally winning the World Series or the Patriots finally winning the Super Bowl. But those moments are way too obvious; we don't need to build an argument for either. Plus, they overlook the joy felt in the more distant past, when the Celtics won all those NBA championships or the Bruins finally won the Stanley Cup.

Instead, we're going with a game that resonates far beyond New England and a moment that will likely never be duplicated in American sports.

The 1980 Olympic hockey game against the Soviet Union.

Oh, we know. We know. Officially, that was a U.S. team, not a Boston team. Heck, more players on that team were from Minnesota than Boston. Doesn't matter. Four of the players were from Massachusetts: Dave Silk and Jack O'Callahan, captain Mike Eruzione, who scored what proved to be the winning goal, and goalkeeper Jim Craig, who shut down the best team in the world.

The Red Sox and Patriots championships lifted New England. The U.S. hockey team lifted the entire nation. America was gripped in seemingly endless inflation and 18 percent interest rates that winter. The Soviets had just invaded Afghanistan. President Carter had recently described a nationwide malaise.

And then this underdog team of hockey players who had been routed by the Soviets in an exhibition game just a month earlier pulled off the greatest upset in American sports history. It wasn't even for the gold medal—the U. S. still had to beat Finland two days later—but it nonetheless was so spectacular a victory that more than 25 years later it still routinely tops any list of the greatest moments in American sports. When the Lake Placid crowd chanted "U-S-A, U-S-A," we echoed their cries from sea to shining sea. When Craig cried on the ice and searched for his father, tears ran down our faces as well. And when Eruzione broke tradition and waved his teammates onto the medal platform, we all leaped up there with them.

What did that moment feel like? Paul Conrad, the political cartoonist for the *Los Angeles Times*, drew a cartoon that captured the moment so perfectly that coach Herb Brooks pinned it up in his office. The cartoon showed the iconic image of the flag-raising on Iwo Jima, only he replaced the Marines with the hockey team and the flag pole with a hockey stick.

The Red Sox may go decades before winning another World Series. New generations of fans may suffer the same pain as their predecessors. Hey, the Celtics might even be good again. But we'll never see anything quite like that hockey game. With the breakup of the Soviet empire and the presence of pro athletes in the Olympics, there never again will be a moment in any sport when the U.S. is such an underdog (and hopefully no moment when an opponent is so hated).

Thanks to some kids from Massachusetts, we not only believed in miracles that night—we believed in our country.

WHAT WAS THE WORST CALL IN BOSTON SPORTS HISTORY?

78 More than any city in North America, maybe even the world, Boston has seen its professional sports teams unfairly maligned by game officials who were either blind, incompetent, or on the take. In some cases all three.

And if you do not believe this assessment, simply ask any Boston sports fan.

The names of evil referees and conspiratorial umpires roll off the lips of angry Boston sports fans, spat out with venom: Larry Barnett. Bill Friday. Jake O'Donnell. Tim Tschida.

And, yes, absolutely, Ben Dreith.

What makes Dreith the villain of villains in Boston sports history is not just that he cost the Patriots a potential playoff victory in 1976, but that he also cost the then-struggling franchise a chance to cement itself as a Boston sports institution—which, as things turned out, did not happen until nearly two decades later.

But the Patriots seemed finally to have arrived in 1976, after many years of either being mediocre or horrifically bad. The '76 Patriots were 11-3 in the regular season, including a 48-17 dismantling of the Oakland Raiders in week four, and the two teams squared off again in the playoffs at the Oakland Coliseum.

Dreith, an official from the original American Football League who moved to the National Football League when the two leagues merged for the 1970 season, was assigned to the game.

With the Patriots leading 21-17 in the fourth quarter, Raiders quarterback Ken Stabler attempted a pass on third-and-18. The pass was incomplete. Here, Dreith etches his name into the New England sports history books. He assessed a head-scratching roughing-the-passer call on Patriots tackle Ray "Sugar Bear" Hamilton, resulting in a first-and-10 for the Raiders at the New England 13.

Four plays later, Stabler went to his left to complete a 1-yard run for an Oakland touchdown. Final score: Raiders 24, Patriots 21.

Replays of the heinous call prove that it was, indeed, heinous. Illegal contact? Not even close.

Prior to the 21st century Patriots winning three Super Bowls in four years, the 1976 team was the best in franchise history, with four Pro Bowlers (tight end Russ Francis, tackle Leon Gray, guard John Hannah, and cornerback Mike Haynes), an exciting scrambler of a quarterback in Steve Grogan, and a sturdy running back in Sam Cunningham.

This was the Patriots' first playoff appearance since the AFL championship game on January 5, 1964, and their first-ever NFL playoff appearance. A Super Bowl victory might have ignited interest in the team; instead, the Pats were doomed to many more years of fighting to be relevant in the Boston sports market.

As for Dreith, he has done little over the years to soothe the feelings of embittered Patriots fans. During a 2002 interview on the "Dennis & Callahan" program on Boston's all-sports WEEI, Dreith spoke reverently of his relationship with Raiders owner Al Davis from their days together in the old AFL. It was yet another bad call by Ben Dreith.

WHAT WAS THE MOST BONEHEADED FRONT OFFICE MOVE IN RED SOX HISTORY?

Surprise! In an amazing upset, the dumbest move wasn't selling Babe Ruth to the Yankees for a handful of beads, confederate money, and Enron stock.

That's because as infamous, horrendous, and damaging as the Ruth sale was, there was some logic behind it. Perhaps not as much logic as greed, but some logic nonetheless. Ruth had been causing problems with the team; there were concerns about his late-night behavior, and there actually was some feeling at the time among a minority of people that owner Harry Frazee was improving his team by getting rid of a troublemaker. Unfortunately, they were a little wrong about that.

Nor was the most boneheaded move trading Jeff Bagwell to the Houston Astros for reliever Larry Andersen. Oh, that was awful, too. The Red Sox led the AL East by 6½ games, Andersen was 37 years old, and he pitched in only 22 innings for the Red Sox before filing for free agency and leaving Boston behind. Bagwell, meanwhile, went on to hit

449 home runs, drive in 1,529 runs, bat .300 six times, play in four All-Star games, and win the 1994 MVP award for the Astros, marks that will possibly take him to the Hall of Fame.

As painful as that trade wound up, at least there was a purpose to it. General manager Lou Gorman thought Boston needed to add a left-hander to the bullpen to preserve its lead. Was that really necessary with a 6½ game lead? Maybe not. Was there a more valuable pitcher available than Andersen? Probably. Did he have to give up Bagwell? No. But at least he was trying to improve the team. Andersen did pitch well (a 1.23 ERA and 25 strikeouts), and the Sox did win the AL East title that season by just two games. So no one was complaining too much while standing in line for playoff tickets.

Still, compare that to general manager Haywood Sullivan in 1981 when he lost Carlton Fisk and Fred Lynn simply because he didn't mail them their contracts on time.

Two of the Red Sox greatest players, Fisk and Lynn might have played their entire careers in Boston except for the most boneheaded move in club history. At the very least they should have played the 1981 season with Boston, when the Sox finished 1½ games behind Milwaukee for the second-half title. Unfortunately, management failed to mail them their 1981 contracts by the required December 20, 1980 deadline. Instead, they put it in the mail two days later. Both players took the case to arbitration, arguing that they should be granted immediate free agency.

211

Fearing he could lose Lynn for nothing, Sullivan traded him before the arbitration ruling, dealing him and Steve Renko to the Angels for Joe Rudi, Frank Tanana and Jim Dorsey. Rudi batted .180 with 24 RBIs in one season with Boston before leaving as a free agent. Tanana was 4-10 and left as a free agent. Dorsey never won a game for Boston. Lynn, who still maintains that he wanted to stay in Boston, played another decade and while never again the star he was with the Red Sox, hit another 182 home runs.

Fisk, meanwhile, won his arbitration hearing and quickly signed with Chicago, where he transposed his jersey number (from 27 to 72) and played the next 14 seasons, piling up 214 home runs and 762 RBIs and winding up in the Hall of Fame. Boston, meanwhile, went through 15 catchers before Fisk's retirement, including Sullivan's son, Marc, whose .186 career batting average in parts of five seasons with the Sox is the very definition of nepotism.

As Annie Savoy says in *Bull Durham*, bad trades are part of baseball. It's one thing to lose a possible future Hall of Famer because you made a bad trade while trying to improve the team. But to lose a future Hall of Famer and an All-Star because of such gross negligence? That's unforgivable.

WHO WAS THE BIGGEST CELTICS VILLAIN?

Bill Laimbeer played 14 seasons in the National Basketball Association, 12 of them with the Detroit Pistons. A big man who blended surprisingly well with the likes of Isiah Thomas and Joe Dumas, he helped lead the Pistons to back-to-back NBA championships in 1989 and '90. By the time he retired he was the Pistons' all-time rebounder, and one of just 19 NBA players to amass 10,000 points and 10,000 rebounds.

And just to show he could handle a clipboard as well as he could handle the paint, Laimbeer coached the Detroit Shock of the Women's National Basketball Association to the league championship in 2003.

But if you run any of these accolades and achievements past your typical Boston Celtics fan, said fan is likely to look at you and say, "And your point is?"

Celtics didn't—and don't—like Bill Laimbeer, and this sentence is delivered in two tenses with the utmost confidence in the belief that His Royal Heinous, as Laimbeer often has been called, would be booed off the court were he to make a guest appearance at the TD Banknorth Garden.

213

Laimbeer made his reputation the old-fashioned way: He clubbed somebody over the head when the refs weren't looking. Add in the elbowing and the flopping, the hip extensions and the flopping, the crying and the flopping, and there you have it: A real, live villain.

Did we mention the flopping?

"That's the thing that fans hated the most about Laimbeer—that he was a flopper," said Glenn Ordway, who, as radio voice of the Celtics in the 80s and early 90s saw a lot of Laimbeer.

"He was a fake," said Ordway. "But he was one of those guys that the hometown fans loved. They loved him in Detroit. They hated him everywhere else."

Isiah Thomas is said to have once told the *Detroit News* that opposing fans "love to hate him."

That may have been true in, say, Dallas or Denver or Milwaukee. It was not true in Boston. Celtics fans chose simply to hate Laimbeer, leaving out the love.

On May 26, 1987, in a playoff game best remembered for Larry Bird stealing an Isiah Thomas inbounds pass with five seconds remaining, a play which led to a Dennis Johnson basket and a 108-107 Boston victory, Celtics center Robert Parish wrapped his fingers into a nice, tight NBA-sized fist and aimed it at Laimbeer. And connected. And as soon as the punch landed, NBA analysts offered three predictions:

Parish was going to get suspended.

Parish was going to get fined.

Parish was going to earn a silent round of applause from virtually every player in the league.

Sure enough, two days later, Parish was suspended from Game 6 in Detroit and fined $7,500, a penalty second only to the $10,000 Kermit Washington was fined for slugging Rudy Tomjanovich in 1977.

"Robert didn't hit people," said Ordway. "It just wasn't his nature. To get him to do something like that, you really had to get him mad. That's what Laimbeer could do to people."

WHO WAS THE BIGGEST RED SOX VILLAIN?

Following the death of President Franklin Delano Roosevelt, a Republican journalist named William Allen White wrote these famous words of FDR: "We who hate your gaudy guts, salute you."

The same could be said by Red Sox fans of legendary New York Yankees slugger Reggie Jackson.

While it's true that Isiah Thomas' quote about Bill Laimbeer being the guy opposing fans "love to hate" does not apply to followers of the Boston Celtics, it works magnificently with Jackson, who very likely heard more boos at

Fenway Park than anyone in the history of the rustic Kenmore Square ballyard.

But booing takes many forms. When you boo your own team's manager for taking a popular pitcher out of the game, that's different than, say, booing an umpire who makes a terrible call, or booing some big bust of a new player who fails to deliver the goods.

Yes, Jackson was booed often and long, booed hard, booed with *feeling*. But there was always a sort of understanding between Red Sox fans and Jackson: He enjoyed the attention, be it in the form of cheers at Yankee Stadium or boos at Fenway Park, and Fenway's fans, in turn, knew they were booing one of the game's great entertainers—as well as one of its most feared clutch hitters.

Look at it another way: Nobody who ever paid to be inside Fenway Park when Jackson was in the lineup ever dared to get a dog or a beer during an inning in which Jackson was due to hit. The logic was simple: You might miss something. And what was amazing about Jackson's presence was that, even in striking out, he did so in memorable, scrapbook-worthy fashion.

Of course, Red Sox fans were acquainted with Jackson long before the future Mr. October ever played a game for the Yankees. Jackson had broken into the big leagues with the old Kansas City Athletics, who soon resettled in Oakland. The A's came into Fenway Park for a June 1969 series against the Red Sox, whereupon Jackson led a three-game Oakland rout of the Sox by going an astonishing 9-for-14 with four home runs and 15 RBI. The A's outscored the Sox 38-13 in the series.

Nine years later, when the Yankees swept a four-game series against the Red Sox in what came to be known as the Boston Massacre, Jackson went just 4-for-16, but it was a loud 4-for-16: He had a home run and drove in six runs. Come October, when the Yankees emerged from a one-game playoff against the Red Sox with a 5-4 victory, it was Jackson's eighth-inning home run off Bob Stanley that proved to be the margin of difference.

Reggie Jackson, still working for the Yankees, and still preening, seems to enjoy visiting Fenway Park. And now, all these years later, aging Sox fans can agree that Jackson's years with the New York Yankees represented a special time in baseball.

They hated him. And loved every minute of it.

WHO WAS THE BIGGEST PATRIOTS VILLAIN?

Jack Tatum has always insisted that that the career-ending hit he threw on New England Patriots wide receiver Darryl Stingley during a 1978 preseason game was strictly business, that it was "a clean hit."

But while that point will forever be debated, we need waste no time playing the point-counterpoint game as pertains to the aftermath of Tatum's hit: Years later, in an attempt to promote an autobiography he had written, Tatum shamelessly attempted to "reach out" to Stingley.

And that, more than the hit itself, is why Jack Tatum, the self-described "Assassin" of the Oakland Raiders, is the biggest villain in Patriots history.

Reach out to Stingley? The only member of the Raiders family who ever reached out to the injured player was the team's coach, John Madden, who frequently visited Stingley while he was staying in a Bay Area hospital.

The hit took place during an August 12, 1978, preseason game between the Patriots and Raiders at the Oakland-Alameda County Coliseum. Stingley, who had run a slant pattern and was leaping for a pass when he was hit by Tatum, suffered a spinal cord injury of such magnitude that he was rendered a paraplegic.

Despite these handicaps, Stingley has gone on to lead a productive life. He eventually returned to Purdue University and earned a degree, then resettled in his native Chicago. Among his many other endeavors is the Chicago-based Darryl Stingley Youth Foundation.

All kinds of stories have made the rounds over the years suggesting that Tatum has tried to visit Stingley, but, as can best be determined, no meeting has ever taken place. But that never stopped Tatum from attempting to capitalize on his reputation as a gridiron tough guy, having authored such books as *Assassin* and *They Still Call Me Assassin*.

Though Tatum has often expressed remorse about the hit, with friends of his suggesting that it remains on his mind to this day, the tough-guy talk has made it difficult for Patriots fans to see him as anything other than the guy who planted a popular player in a wheelchair. (Tatum, who suffers from diabetes, would eventually have his left leg amputated below the knee.)

Boston Herald columnist Joe Fitzgerald, writing in 1996, said of Tatum, "He's surely no favorite at this address." Fitzgerald apparently could not get past this quote from Tatum in *They Still Call Me Assassin:* "I never made a tackle just to bring someone down. I want to punish the man I'm going after. I like to believe my best hits border on felonious assault."

Understand that the search for mean and nasty things that have been written about Jack Tatum needn't be limited to the Boston media. In a 1992 article in the *San Francisco Chronicle*, writer Andrew Postman had this to say about Jack Tatum: "Thirteen years after delivering his paralysis-inducing hit on New England Patriots wide receiver Darryl Stingley, former Oakland Raiders defensive back (Jack) Tatum still inspires disgust."

WHO WAS THE BIGGEST BRUINS VILLAIN?

As the never-ending battle between good and evil is so much a part of hockey, with its rich brawling tradition and a subspecies of player aptly known as the "goon," it came as no surprise that there were many contenders for the title of biggest villain in Bruins history.

Where to begin? How about Wayne Maki? During an exhibition game in 1969, Maki, a forward with the St. Louis Blues, got into a horrific stick-swinging fight with Bruins tough guy Ted Green. The result: Green suffered a fractured skull that kept him out the entire season.

Remember Pat Quinn? Long before he gained fame as the jowly, ruddy-faced coach of several NHL teams, Quinn was a menacing defenseman who in 1969, as a member of the Toronto Maple Leafs, knocked Bruins great Bobby Orr unconscious with a body check during a first-round play-off game.

The Bruins have suffered many a playoff loss to the Montreal Canadiens over the years, which, naturally, means there are many Canadiens villains. Chief among them is John Ferguson, whose beating of the aforementioned Ted Green in Game 1 of a 1968 Bruins-Canadiens playoff series set the tempo for a four-game sweep by the Habs.

Yet these people form a collection of choir boys when placed alongside Ulf Samuelsson, who absolutely is the biggest villain in Bruins history. Look at it this way: Ted Green recovered from his stick-swinging incident with Maki and returned to playing hockey. (And, anyway, let's remember that Green was always up for a good fight.) Orr, too, recovered from the check by Quinn, and, it should be noted, beat the guy up a couple of times.

But Samuelsson, one of hockey's most hated cheap-shot artists, brought Neely's career to a premature end. He took out Neely with an open-ice, leg-extension hit in Game 3 of the 1991 Wales Conference finals.

After taking another shot from Samuelsson in the deciding sixth game of the series, Neely was later diagnosed with myositis ossificans, which caused a portion of his left thigh muscle to turn to bone. Neely played only 22 games over the next two seasons; though he made a comeback during the 1993-94 season, scoring 50 goals in 49 games, the extent of the injury was such that he was done by the end of the 1995-96 season. He was just 31 when his career ended.

In his column in the November 3, 1991 *Boston Globe*, Kevin Paul Dupont summed up Ulf Samuelsson rather succinctly, writing that he ". . . starts the fire and then moves away for others to stamp out the flames. If you don't know his number, take a look at the Pittsburgh bench. He'll be the one sitting there, getting challenged by an opponent to get back out on the ice and finish what he started. Of

221

course, that never happens."

The way Bruins fans see it, bygones will never be bygones where Ulf Samuelsson is concerned. He is, and always will be, a Bruins villain.

WHAT WAS THE BEST MOMENT IN RED SOX HISTORY, FINALLY WINNING THE WORLD SERIES OR BEATING THE YANKEES IN THE PLAYOFFS?

84 The question sounds absurd at first. How much better could things be? Boston won the friggin' World Series! The city had waited 86 miserable years for that to happen. This was what everyone had dreamed about for generations. There is no way that moment could be topped. It's like saying, "What was better, sleeping with Angelina Jolie or seeing her in a matinee of *Alexander*?" Don't be stupid.

And yet. . . .

And yet how could anything be more satisfying than when Dave Roberts stole the bag off Mariano Rivera and the Red Sox rallied in the ninth inning and David Ortiz went deep in the 12th inning to win Game 4 and send Boston on to the most improbable comeback in baseball history? As one fan shouted as he left Fenway Park that night, "I'm going to dance in the streets and hug strangers."

That initial dance went on three more nights, with the shelf-life of "Greatest Game in Red Sox History" lasting approximately 24 hours. The very next night after his 12th-inning walkoff home run, Big Papi topped it with a walkoff single in the 14th inning to win Game 5. Then Curt Schilling became the living symbol of the Red Sox when he took the mound despite a bleeding ankle and shut down the Yankees in Game 6. The Red Sox still needed another victory at Yankee Stadium (a site where they never, ever win when it matters) and yet everyone knew New York was already defeated long before Johnny Damon's grand slam in Game 7. We knew it the moment A-Rod slapped pathetically at Bronson Arroyo and how good did watching that make you feel?

The Red Sox finally defeated the Yankees with the pennant on the line, becoming the first team in baseball history to rally from an 0-3 series deficit. God, does it get any better than that?

"Tonight is about winning the American League and going through the Yankees to do it," Theo Epstein said in the clubhouse that night. "This is for all the great Red Sox teams and players that would have been in the World

Series if it hadn't been for the Yankees. The 1949 team, 1978, 1999, last year. This is for all the fans who would have been able to go to the World Series if it hadn't been for the Yankees."

People immediately said the alleged Curse of the Bambino was over, even though, one, there never was a curse, and two, even if there was, the Sox still had to win the World Series to end it. But that seemed almost a foregone conclusion after the Sox had rallied against the Evil Empire. Hell, Boston was on such a roll, they not only swept the Cardinals in four games, they became the first team in World Series history to hold a lead in every inning of the series.

The World Series was so swift, so overwhelming, so easy that it was almost anti-climactic after the comeback against the Yankees. Almost. The ALCS might seem more satisfying to some but without the World Series victory, it would have been just another setup to another painful Red Sox punchline. Instead, the two formed the greatest 11 days in Red Sox history.

That's why, no matter how good it felt finally shutting up those damn Yankees fans, winning the World Series was more satisfying. "The best part of this is all those Red Sox fans don't have anything to be upset about anymore," Doug Mientkiewicz said on the field after Game 4 of the World Series. "They don't have to be depressed and wait for something bad to happen. They can smile and be happy."

WHO WAS FENWAY'S GREATEST ALL-TIME ANTHEM SINGER?

The list of singers who have performed the national anthem at Fenway Park reads like a who's who of American entertainment.

Lou Rawls sang the national anthem at Fenway. So did James Taylor and Steven Tyler, as well as the Cowsills and the Kingston Trio. Smoky Robinson did an anthem, as did Judy Collins. Ray Charles once sang "America the Beautiful."

Yet the most beautiful, most uplifting national anthem ever performed at the crusty, old Kenmore Square ballyard was delivered by a four-year-old boy named Jordan Leandre, a Massachusetts native who in 2001 was diagnosed with Ewing's sarcoma, a form of bone cancer usually found in children and young adults.

As he battled his cancer, Jordan, an optimistic, forward-looking little fellow, sought ways to deal with the upheaval in his lifestyle. One way, he found, was to learn how to sing "The Star Spangled Banner," his plan being that he would perform the anthem before one of his older brother Andrew's Babe Ruth League games.

225

He did just that, and soon, while undergoing treatment at Boston's famed Dana-Farber Cancer Institute, his talent was brought to the attention of the Red Sox. Jordan, perhaps the biggest Red Sox fan in New England, was only too pleased to strut his stuff at Fenway Park.

But you don't go directly from the Babe Ruth League to the big leagues. The Red Sox, ever-watchful of their prospects, brought the kid along slowly. First, he took part in a new-fangled Fenway Park ritual in which a little tyke leans into a microphone behind home plate and beseeches the combatants from both teams to, "Play ball!"

On August 26, 2004, Jordan sang his first Fenway anthem. What he lacked in formal training and pitch was more than made up for in style. To watch Jordan sing the national anthem, and to do so with such unbridled optimism and passion, is to be reminded of man's (in this case, child's) unique gift for being able to overcome adversity.

"I know it will sound like I'm just saying this because he's my son, but he has a special gift," said Jordan's father, Ken Leandre. "People will come up to him in the supermarket and just start talking to him.

"He finds a silver lining in everything," he said. "If something's broke, he just says, 'Let's get a new one.' He's touched so many people's lives."

As of the All-Star break in 2006, Jordan had performed the national anthem at Fenway Park on seven occasions. As such, he has formed a bond with several Red Sox sluggers, notably David Ortiz. The Red Sox say they never endeavored to bring the two together, that their friendship simply evolved over time.

Jordan has yet another talent: An ability to speak his mind. He once told Red Sox first baseman Kevin Millar to stop striking out so much.

As of the summer of 2006, Jordan Leandre was winning his battle against the cancer. The next hurdle is to save his legs; a series of operations was planned as this book went to press.

WHAT WAS THE LOWEST MOMENT IN RED SOX HISTORY?

The Bucky Dent and Aaron Boone games were shotgun blasts to the gut. They were painful, near lethal attacks to the body that left ugly, jagged wounds not even Big Papi could fully heal. But as bad as they were, the loss to the Mets was worse.

That's because the Red Sox were so close to finally winning it all and ending 68 years of misery that you could read the fine print pregnancy warnings on the champagne bottle labels. This was literally so in the Boston clubhouse, where crews already had hung plastic curtains over the lockers to protect the clothing from the champagne spray. NBC broadcaster Bob Costas was in the clubhouse to interview the Red Sox about their victory. The MVP award was ready for Bruce Hurst.

Despite entering the 1986 World Series as considerable underdogs, the Red Sox held a two-run lead with two out and nobody on in the bottom of the 10th inning that night. Closer Calvin Schiraldi needed just one more out to clinch Boston's first world championship since 1918. The Mets were so down that first baseman Keith Hernandez was back in the clubhouse drinking a beer and Kevin Mitchell was making travel reservations, both fully convinced that the series was over. The Shea Stadium scoreboard even flashed a message reading, "Congratulations Red Sox, 1986 World Series Champions!"

Throughout New England, and indeed, around the country, Red Sox fans are ready to celebrate. And surely in more than one bar, a friend turns to another and says, "This is it. After all these years, you're finally going to win." And surely in more than one bar, the friend replies cautiously, "It's not over yet."

No, it isn't. Gary Carter singles.

Well, no problem. We'll get the next guy.

And then Mitchell, pinch hitting for Rick Aguilera, singles to put the tying run on first.

Hey, still nothing to worry about. Just got to get one more out. In fact, just one more strike. We got an 0-2 count on Ray Knight.

Knight singles, scoring Carter.

OK, getting a little nervous here but c'mon, we only need the one out. We're still gonna win. At least Schiraldi is out and we've got Bob Stanley in there now. The old Stanley Steamer. C'mon, Steamer! You got two strikes on Mookie Wilson. Put him away! Just one more strike, one more strike!

Stanley throws a pitch to the backstop, scoring Mitchell with the tying run and moving Knight to second base.

Dammit! I knew it! I knew it! They're screwing it up! They're gonna lose!!!

Mookie Wilson hits a dribbler down the first base line, Bill Buckner bends down to field it and ...

AWWWWGGGGGGGGGHHHHHHH!!!!!!

Not that the misery ended there. Oh, no. The Red Sox merely had to win Game 7 and the sun would rise again. A rainout even gave Boston a day to recover from the loss. The Red Sox certainly seemed to be back on track the next night when they took an early 3-0 lead.

Hey, it's gonna be all right after all. Just a little scare is all. A last reminder of what it's like to root for the Red Sox.

And then Jim Rice is thrown out at second base on what should be a routine double. And then the Mets tie the game. And then Ray Knight homers. And then ... well, the rest is too painful to write.

There have been many miserable losses in Red Sox history, losses so painful that future generations will be forced to take ulcer medicine for them, but that was the worst.

Never before had the Red Sox been (and hopefully never again will be) so close to winning it all only to lose in the end. One little out was all they needed. One measly strike.

Curses, indeed.

WHY GINO CAPPELLETTI BELONGS IN THE PRO FOOTBALL HALL OF FAME

87 According to its web site, the Pro Football Hall of Fame ". . . serves as a hallowed honoring spot for the greats of the pro football world."

For the purposes of this discussion, the important word in that sentence is "pro," as in professional. In other words, enshrinement in the Pro Football Hall of Fame is not limited to players from the National Football League.

Remember the American Football League? The late, great AFL served as a rustic, seat-of-its-pants alternative to the powerful National Football League for 10 years until the two leagues merged in 1970, yet even before the merger the AFL and NFL squared off in the fledgling Super Bowl as early as 1967.

Yet despite the merger, history has not always been kind to the AFL. Some of the league's greatest players have faded from memory, their accomplishments, their successes, their records now just the stuff of microfilm, scrapbooks, and the fuzzy anecdotes of old-timers.

Which brings us to Gino Cappelletti, a longtime Patriot from the days of the American Football League. He remains popular and well known in New England through his many years as a color analyst on the Patriots' radio network, but younger fans may not know—or even care—that he was one of the team's first great performers.

Cappelletti, who served double duty as a wide receiver and place kicker, joined the Patriots for their inaugural season in 1960. Eleven years later, when the Pats played their first season in the NFL, Cappelletti was still around, closing out a distinguished 11-year career.

One of just three men to play in every game in the ten-year history of the AFL, Cappelletti was a five-time AFL All-Star pick, the equivalent of being named All-Pro. He led the AFL in scoring five times, including the two best scoring seasons in AFL history, with 155 points in 1964 and 147 in 1961.

Even today, many years after the AFL-NFL merger, and with the Patriots having made five appearances in the Super Bowl (winning three of them), Cappelletti's name still appears among the team's all-time scoring leaders. His 1,130 points trail only Adam Vinatieri's 1,158. He's second to Vinatieri in PAT kicks and field goals made, and his six field goals in a game (October 4, 1964, against Denver) is still a franchise record.

In 1971, Gino Cappelletti was named to the All-AFL tenth anniversary team. He is among 11 players enshrined in the Patriots' Hall of Fame, and the team has long since retired his No. 20. Yet Gino Cappelletti has yet to be enshrined in Canton, Ohio, home of the Pro Football Hall of Fame.

This is one player whose successes are not hidden away on aging spools of microfilm. Every stat, every accomplishment can be found on page 301 of the Patriots' 2006 media guide.

The writers who decide which players get into the Pro Football Hall of Fame . . . do they get a Patriots media guide each season?

If so, do they read it?

DID THE RED SOX GIVE NOMAR GARCIAPARRA THE BUM'S RUSH?

What the Kennedy family is to state politics, Nomar and his idiosyncrasies were to Boston sports. Kids throughout New England copied his nervous tics at the plate—adjust the right wrist band, adjust the left wrist band, kick the dirt, adjust the right wrist band, steam-press his uniform pants, signal for the peanut vendor, request a pedicure—while so many fans worshipped him that *Saturday Night Live* built a series of sketches around the cult of Nomah.

So what happened? Did the Red Sox shove him out the door? Or did Nomar open the door himself, petulantly step outside, and only then realize he was on the third floor?

The once-loving relationship started unraveling in 2003 when Nomar and the Red Sox couldn't quite agree on four-year, $60 million contract offer (well detailed in Seth Mnookin's *Feeding the Monster*). Given that the offer was substantially less than Alex Rodriguez or Derek Jeter had recently received, Nomar wanted more in the form of a signing bonus. The Red Sox didn't want to give it to him. The situation worsened when the Sox tried pulling off the ludicrous A-Rod trade, alienating their best and most popular player, with whom they were supposedly still in negotiations. Generally speaking, this is not a good approach to woo a client. Nomar was so upset by the trade attempt that he called radio station WEEI during his Hawaiian honeymoon to say he wanted to stay in Boston.

(And Mia must have *loved* that call. *"Come to bed Nomar. I'm wearing that little silk negligee you gave me."*

"Just a minute honey. I'm on hold for Dale and Neumie.")

Things just got worse from there. Understandably, Nomar showed up to spring training in a bad mood and

233

began what would become the team record for most consecutive days pouting at a locker. When he sat out a game in Yankee Stadium to nurse an injury (while Jeter, fresh from a meeting of the Justice League of America, was diving into the stands after foul balls), the Red Sox decided they had to trade him.

They really didn't have much choice at that point, given that Nomar wasn't completely healthy and probably was going to sign elsewhere as a free agent after the season. And obviously, the trade worked out for the Red Sox, with Orlando Cabrera playing great defense while batting .294 with six home runs down the stretch (and even better in the postseason).

But that's not really the issue. The issue is whether both sides could have handled everything better so that Nomar could have stayed happy and productive in Boston (or failing that, been traded for more than two players who were also going to leave as free agents). Just because the Red Sox won the World Series after they traded Nomar doesn't mean they couldn't have also won the series with a happy Nomar in the lineup.

Nomar is as much to blame as the Red Sox for how things ended. But when a player is that good and had been that popular, both sides should have been able to work out a contract that could have given Boston the world championship in 2004 plus keep one of the game's best hitters in the lineup for 2005, 2006, 2007, 2008 and beyond. . . .

COULD THE BULLPEN BY COMMITTEE STRATEGY HAVE WORKED?

Yes. And more importantly, the Red Sox should go back to it again, especially if Jon Papelbon goes to the rotation.

Admittedly, the decision to defy current baseball wisdom by going with a closer by committee didn't work so well when the Red Sox squandered several leads early in the 2003 season. The team eventually was forced to bow to convention.

But was the real problem the strategy or the pitchers the Sox used within it?

Before you answer, consider this. A study that ran in an old edition of *Total Baseball* closely examined late-inning leads from three distinct eras of relief strategy—1952, 1972, and 1992. It looked at every lead of three runs or less from the eighth inning on, and what it found was that despite the rise of closers and the eventual reliance on them, there wasn't much difference in how successfully a team protected a close lead late in the game.

That's right. Whether they stayed with their starter or went with several different relievers or relied on a specific closer, teams pretty much won the same percentage of games. No matter the relief strategy used, teams that held a lead in the eighth inning or later usually won. The key was not who you had pitching with a lead in the eighth and ninth inning; the key was making sure you got to there with the lead.

Statistical analysis repeatedly shows that it is more valuable for teams to use their best reliever when the game is close earlier in the game rather than waiting until the ninth inning just so the closer can build his resume with an easy save. Anyone can save a game when they enter the ninth inning with a three-run lead. Why hold your best reliever for such a situation that might arise in the ninth inning when you're in more jeopardy of losing a lead in the sixth or seventh? Unless you stop the rally then, there may not be a lead in the ninth inning or a precious save opportunity to worry about.

That's really what Theo meant by the "closer by committee" strategy, anyway. "We still want a truly dominant reliever (or two, or three, or four). We just won't hold him back for the ninth inning so he can chalk up a save," he said in a BostonDirtdogs.com chat. "The goal is to put the best pitcher in the game to get the most critical outs, period."

Furthermore, despite everything you always hear about the importance of having a proven closer and the special "makeup" required for such pitchers, teams don't seem to have that much problem finding someone who can do the job fairly well for a season or two. Keith Foulke handled the position well enough to win a World Series. Then Papelbon replaced him quite well. And someone down the road will follow him as well. Hell, Tom Gordon once was so highly prized that Stephen King wrote a novel using him as a key figure.

Why does it make a difference what relief strategy the Red Sox used a couple years ago? Because they and other teams routinely overpay closers millions of dollars to protect three-run leads in the ninth inning when that money would be far better invested in starters or position players.

That's why they should move Papelbon to the rotation. As good as he was as a closer for much of 2006, the rookie might have been even more valuable had he been starting when the Red Sox so clearly needed another arm in the rotation. As it was, Papelbon blew six save chances from June to the end of August while saving just 15 games, hardly a great ratio. And then he wound up with a sore shoulder and missed all of September anyway. Would he have stayed healthy if he had been a starter? We don't know. But the Sox might have won more games had he pitched at the front end of some games rather at the end, when the outcomes were mostly decided.

By using their best pitchers earlier in the game and wisely investing their "closer" money on other players, the Red Sox will build the all-important leads more often and win more games. The only person who loses out is the overpaid closer.

And, of course, his agent.

WHAT ARE THE BEST BOSTON SPORTS MOVIES?

90 The best sports movies usually are set outside the big cities, well away from $10 ticket prices and $6 popcorn. The best baseball movie? A tossup between *Bull Durham* (Durham, North Carolina) and *Field of Dreams* (small-town Iowa). The best basketball movie? *Hoosiers* (small-town Indiana). The best hockey movie? *Slapshot* (Charlestown, West Virginia). The best cycling movie? *Breaking Away* (Bloomington, Indiana).

So, it's no surprise that the best Boston sports moments come in movies that aren't about sports. The 2005 version of *War of the Worlds* is a modern allegory between the forces of good and utter evil, which is exemplified early on when the Tom Cruise character plays catch with his son. Tom dons a Yankees cap; his boy retaliates by defiantly slipping a Red Sox cap on his head. The son doesn't have a pleasant time when the Martians land and start killing everyone with heat lasers, but at least he meets a better fate than Tim Robbins does when he wears a Red Sox cap in *Mystic River*.

Anyway, our top five:

5. *The Babe*. What's the difference between *The Babe*, which came out in 1993, and *Babe*, which came out two years later? One movie tells the story of a pig's adventures when it's forced to go to the big city. The other one has talking animals. Seriously though, it was tough deciding whether this belonged on the best movie list or the worst. It has a very nice take on Ruth, with Goodman capturing how the Babe's larger-than-life appetite for everything stemmed from deep vulnerability. This could have been a great movie had Goodman not weighed 60 pounds too much or had they not needlessly deviated from the facts with ridiculous scenes like Ruth hitting a popup so high that he circles the bases for a home run before the ball lands in the infield. We mean, if ever a person's life did not require embellishing, it was Ruth's.

4. *Miracle*. This impeccably realistic story of the 1980 Olympic hockey team focuses on coach Herb Brooks, but we also get a look at the intense rivalry between the Minnesota and Greater Boston players that climaxes at the end of a brutal workout when they come together. "I'm Mike Eruzione," the team captain says, "and I play for the United States of America."

3. *Field of Dreams*. Not exactly a Boston movie, but there is the marvelous scene when Kevin Costner kidnaps James Earl Jones and takes him to a Red Sox

239

game. For some people, the ultimate movie experience is seeing Gene Kelly tap-dancing through a rainstorm, or Bogie telling Ingrid Bergman that if she doesn't get on that plane she'll regret it for the rest of her life, or Angelina Jolie slipping into some black leather. For us, it's seeing the Green Monster on the silver screen.

2. *St. Ralph.* A relatively unknown but tenderly funny movie about a teen who decides he must cure his mother of cancer through a miracle—winning the Boston Marathon, even though he's never run a race of any distance. With a plot like that, you expect it to be filled with every scene from the Official Sports Movie Book of Clichés. Instead, it's endearingly quirky, unconventional, and very enjoyable.

1. *Good Will Hunting.* Yeah, yeah. Lou Merloni's favorite actor not only appears in it, he co-wrote it as well. And it's not about sports. But so what? For all the work *Fever Pitch* went to explain the balancing act between the love of a woman and the love of the Sox, no scene better captures this as well (and as effortlessly) as *GWH* does when Robin Williams explains how he gave up a ticket to Game 6 of the 1975 World Series so he could stay in a bar and introduce himself to his future wife.

Damon, as Will, tells Williams that he can't understand how he could give up a ticket to the greatest game in Red Sox history (remember, this movie was filmed in 1997) and Williams, as his counselor Sean, responds that it was all worth it—"You should have seen this girl. She lit up the room."—then goes on to say he doesn't regret the decision nor their 18 years of marriage nor any of the sacrifices he made in the six years when his wife was dying nor all that she added to his life. "And I sure as hell don't regret missing that game."

Visibly impressed by Sean's emotional response, Will doesn't say anything for awhile. Finally he comments, "Would have been nice to catch the game, though."

"Well, hell," Sean replies, "I didn't know Pudge was gonna hit the home run."

Still gives us goosebumps.

WHAT ARE THE WORST BOSTON SPORTS MOVIES?

There have been relatively few Boston sports movies. Sadly, a significant percentage of them were bad. We give these five two thumbs down, way down.

5. *Fear Strikes Out.* The best thing about *The Natural* is that once it set the standard, all future baseball movies had to get the baseball right. Unlike this 1957 movie, where some of the Red Sox games are played among palm trees. It's interesting as a study of parental pressure and psychosis but is so over-wrought and melodramatic it's almost laughable. And if you ever wondered whether any actor could show form worse than Tim Robbins in *Bull Durham* just watch Anthony Perkins. You keep waiting for him to carve up Ted and stick him in the attic.

4. *Fever Pitch.* The Farrelly brothers are huge Red Sox fans and know their comedy and their baseball. There is a very good scene when Jimmy Fallon sees several Red Sox at a table laughing after a loss and realizes that the fans care more about winning and losing than the players. The problem, though, is too enormous to over-come. You never can accept Fallon cast as a real Red Sox fan. This is the worst casting decision since Francis Ford Coppola put his daughter, Sofia, in *Godfather III*.

3. *Karate Kid 4: The Next Karate Kid.* Awful. The only thing you can say for this Boston-set pile is that Mr. Myagi is a better trainer than Clint Eastwood because Hilary Swank doesn't wind up getting killed in this one.

2. *Amazing Grace and Chuck.* Can you imagine the pitch meeting for this movie? "OK, here's the plot. A Little League pitcher named Chuck sees a Minuteman

missile and announces that he's not to pitch until there is a complete nuclear disarmament. A Boston Celtic player—I'm thinking of using Alex English because of his complete lack of acting experience—reads about him and decides to join the cause. Then he and some Miami Dolphins join Chuck in his barn and won't play unless the U.S. and Soviets agree to disarm. And then an arms dealer blows up English on a plane. And just when it looks like the baseball season will be cancelled, President Gregory Peck and the Russians agree to lay down their weapons.

And you thought the Red Sox' 2004 championship was improbable?

1. *Celtic Pride.* Here's the plot: With the NBA finals heading into Game 7, Jimmy (Dan Akroyd) and Mike (Daniel Stern) kidnap Utah Jazz star Lewis Scott (Damon Wayons) to ensure that the Celtics win the championship in the final game at the old Garden. This movie might have worked in different hands, but instead you'll be rooting for the Garden to be imploded before it ends—with Akroyd and Stern inside.

DO THE RED SOX LEFT FIELDERS REPRESENT BASEBALL'S GREATEST POSITION DYNASTY?

92 Other teams go through left fielders the way Italy goes through governments. Not the Red Sox. You might as well wait for a Supreme Court justice to die or get in line at the end of the cue for Space Mountain during spring break. Playing left field in Boston is almost an inherited position, passed down from player to player as judiciously and sparingly as an English peerage or season tickets to the Packers.

From Ted to Manny, no other team has produced such a royal blood-line of talent at one position. Sox left fielders have produced 42 All-Star nods, 10 batting titles, nine home run championships, four MVP awards, three Triple Crowns and two Hall of Fame plaques (so far). It isn't an absolute requisite that Boston left fielders hit .300 with 30 home runs and 100 RBIs every season, but it helps.

The only serious challenge to this positional dynasty is center fielder for the Yankees, which has been home to its own lineage of great players, including DiMaggio, Mickey Mantle, and Bernie Williams.

Add up the awards and production of the Yankees center fielders, and the two positions are pretty close. What distinguishes Boston's left fielders over New York's center fielders, however, is the purity of the lineage. Weed out the war and injury years, and Fenway's famous left field has been ruled by just five players—Williams, Yaz, Rice, Mike Greenwell, and Manny. Sure, Tommy Harper played there in 1973 and Troy O'Leary was there from 1998-2000, but hey, Joan Rivers has guest-hosted *The Tonight Show* but no one considers her one of the show's four core hosts. Excluding Ted's war years, there were only four seasons (1997-2000) in which one member of the Fab Five did not play some games in left field, and only eight seasons in which one of them was not the Sox everyday left fielder.

The Yankees, meanwhile, went through a dozen center fielders over the course of 27 seasons between Mantle and Williams. Some of those center fielders were quite good (Rickey Henderson played two years there) and several more were not (Ron Woods, Ruppert Jones, Omar Moreno), but none were New York's regular center fielder for more than four seasons. In the 17 seasons from 1965 to 1981, the Yankees went through nine regular center fielders.

Taking up residence in front of the Green Monster is like moving into the Vatican. Not many people are deemed worthy enough to do so, and those that are tend to stay awhile. There essentially have been more Popes (six) in that span than regular Red Sox left fielders.

245

One more way playing left field at Fenway is better than playing center field at Yankee Stadium? You don't have to duck as many bottles.

WHAT ARE THE MOST OVERPRICED SEATS IN BASEBALL?

93 At 56 stories, the Montparnasse Tower is the tallest skyscraper in Paris. It's also the most hated building in Paris due to its horrid, modern, glass office tower design. And yet the view level of the Montparnasse Tower is one of the most popular tourist sites in a city that boasts the Eiffel Tower, Notre Dame, Montmartre, the Musee Dorsay, and the Louvre. Why? Because it offers virtually the same view as the top of the Eiffel Tower does with the notable differences that:

1. You can see the Eiffel Tower,

and more importantly,

2. You can't see the Montparnasse Tower.

We mention this as an introduction to our argument on the incredibly popular seats atop the Green Monster. Introduced in 2003, the Green Monster seats go for an average of $110—or at least that's the average price the Red Sox were selling them for in 2006 to the privileged few able to snag them. The rest of us have to rely on the secondary market. We just searched on eBay for a Yankees series in August and two seats were going for $360 with a day left in the bidding. Excuse us, did we say seats? We meant tickets, because that was $360 for standing room. Want a seat? Someone else was asking $1,500 for a pair.

Now, there's no doubt that being on top of the Monster is very, very cool indeed. They aren't just seats; they're part of a treasured landmark. Unless you actually play left field for the Red Sox, this is as close to being a part of history as you can get. Watching the Red Sox from atop the Green Monster must be like watching a Fourth of July fireworks display from Abraham Lincoln's forehead at Mount Rushmore. Plus, you have access to a private concession stand.

There's only one drawback to the Monster seats. The view.

Remember, when you're on top of the Monster, you're not only a football field away from home plate, you're also 37 feet above the field. Unless you're in the front row, you can't see the left fielder catch deep fly balls. Forget the history involved: When you get right down to it, we're really talking about view-obstructed outfield seats that sell for hundreds of dollars.

Worst of all, you can't see the very thing that makes Fenway famous—the Green Monster itself.

The seats in right field are a much better bargain. For one thing, they sell for $45, a savings of at least $55 over the Monster seats, or enough money to buy a hot dog and two beers. They're also much lower to the field, with many so close that a Yankees right fielder can actually hear every foul syllable of your curses.

Most importantly, they give you a terrific view of baseball's most important piece of architecture: the Monster.

WAS THE 1975 WORLD SERIES THE BEST EVER PLAYED?

Writers occasionally refer to the 1975 World Series as the best ever played, and with good argument. There are still New Englanders waiting for their cuticles to grow back all the way.

But after more than 100 World Series, the title Greatest Ever is a demanding one. And the series that poses the most serious challenge to 1975 is the 1991 worst-to-first series between the Minnesota Twins and the Atlanta Braves. Let's see how they stack up against each other.

TENSION

Both the 1975 and 1991 series had games as tight as David Ortiz in Pedro's pants. Five games in 1975 were decided by one run. Four times the winning run scored in one team's final at-bat. Two games went into extra innings. Five games in 1991 were decided by one run. Five times the winning run scored in a team's final at-bat. Three games went into extra innings. Edge to 1991.

CONTROVERSY

Both series had interference plays that may have tipped the outcome and resulted in death threats for one of the participants—the Ed Armbrister play in 1975 and the Kent Hrbek WWE wrasslin' move on Ron Gant in 1991. Push.

DRAMA

Both series went down to the wire in Games 6 and 7. Both had extra inning, walkoff home runs in Game 6—future Hall of Famer Carlton Fisk in the 12th inning and future Hall of Famer Kirby Puckett in the 11th. Very slight edge to 1975 for Fisk's body language that provided one of the greatest moments in baseball history.

VENUE

While Riverfront Stadium and Fulton County Stadium are virtual washes, Fenway wins in a rout over the Metrodome. Edge to 1975.

STAR POWER

The 1975 World Series had the better players, with five Hall of Famers (Yaz, Fisk, Joe Morgan, Johnny Bench, Tony

Perez), plus Pete Rose and Luis Tiant (who still might make the Hall). The 1991 World Series has just one Hall of Famer so far (Puckett), though Tom Glavine will almost certainly make it two, while Jack Morris and John Smoltz could eventually make it four. (Jim Rice, remember, did not play in 1975 due to his injury.) The Big Red Machine also was among the greatest teams in history. On the other hand, no one knew it at the time but 1991 was the start of the great Atlanta dynasty that would win a division title every full season for 14 years. Edge: 1975.

INTANGIBLES

We remember talking with Peter Gammons the morning of Game 7 of the 1991 World Series about how the series stacked up with 1975. After a thoughtful discussion, we agreed that the 1991 series needed Game 7 to be decided dramatically in the final innings. And that's precisely what happened. Few moments in postseason history have matched Jack Morris stomping out to the mound for the tenth inning of Game 7. Just miles from his boyhood home in St. Paul, Morris pitched a 10-inning 1-0 shutout that ranks among the great pitching performances in postseason history and the longest outing by a World Series pitcher since Babe Ruth went 14 innings in Game 2 of the 1916 series. Edge: 1991.

So which series gets the edge? For sheer baseball drama, then, we go with 1991. Barely. Though for sheer marquee effect, we won't complain if you pick 1975.

INCH FOR INCH, WHAT WAS THE BIGGEST HIT IN RED SOX HISTORY?

Hint: Carlton Fisk didn't hit it.

Neither did Ted Williams.

Nor did Carl Yastrzemski, David Ortiz, Bill Mueller, Dave Henderson, nor Johnny Damon.

Another hint: inch-for-inch, the most important hit in Red Sox history didn't sail over the Green Monster. Or smack against the Wall. Or curve inside the Pesky Pole. Or drop safely into center field. In fact, it didn't even make it to the infield dirt.

That's because the most important hit in Red Sox history—inch-for-inch—was a bunt. By pitcher Jim Lonborg in the final game of the regular season in 1967.

Wait, hear us out, especially you younger readers.

We've already established the importance of the 1967 season to the Red Sox fate (see argument 28). Well, that season came down to the final Sunday of the season, when the Twins and Red Sox were tied for first place with the Tigers a half-game behind. The Tigers played a double-header against the Angels that day, while the Sox and Twins played at Fenway. Lonborg, 21-9, started for the Red Sox but fell behind 2-0 in the third. The Sox still trailed 2-0 when Lonborg was scheduled to lead off the bottom of the sixth inning. Rather than go to a pinch-hitter, manager Dick Williams chose to stay with the eventual Cy Young winner, despite his .141 batting average.

"Bobby Doerr had worked with me a lot to help me win more ballgames," Lonborg remembers. "He said the way to win more games is to be able to help yourself at the plate so the manager has confidence you can be something more than an automatic out. So I practiced bunting a lot and I was a pretty good baserunner for someone tall.

"When I was in the on-deck circle, I noticed that third baseman Cesar Tovar was playing back at normal position—they didn't think I would bunt—so there was a lot of room there to work with."

Lonborg dropped down a beauty. Tovar had a brief play at it but Lonborg beat it out to start the rally. Three singles, two wild pitches, a fielder's choice, a walk, and an error later, the Red Sox led 5-2. Minnesota closed the gap with another run but got no closer. Lonborg went the distance for a 5-3 win that clinched the pennant.

Had it not been for Lonborg's bunt, there's a good chance the Red Sox would not have rallied that inning and a good chance they would have lost the game. And had they lost the game, they would have finished in second place. And had that happened, everyone would have said, well, that was a nice run but the Sox failed in the end as usual. And they would have gone right back to rooting for the Bruins and Celtics.

Instead, the Sox won much more than the pennant; they won the hearts and minds of Boston. Baseball in Boston never was the same again. Never has a ball that traveled so little brought so much joy to so many fans.

Sometimes, the little plays are just as important as the mighty home runs.

Ask Dave Roberts.

WHAT WAS THE BIGGEST UPSET IN BOSTON SPORTS?

96

In 1903, the Red Sox (then known as the Americans), representing the upstart American League, whipped the Pittsburgh Pirates and the great Honus Wagner in the first World Series. Boston College lost 54-7 to Notre Dame in 1992 but came back the next season to upset the undefeated and No. 1-ranked Irish 41-39—the first time Notre Dame had ever lost to another Catholic school. The 2001 Patriots began the season as 75-1 underdogs to win the championship and entered the Super Bowl as 14-point underdogs to the St. Louis Rams . . . and won 20-17 behind Tom Brady's arm and Adam Vinatieri's foot.

But none of those upsets were the biggest in Boston history. For one thing, due to Pittsburgh's many injuries, Boston was actually a slight favorite by the first pitch of the 1903 World Series. Boston College may have been routed by Notre Dame in 1992, but the Eagles brought a seven-game winning streak into South Bend the next year—they were a pretty good team. And in retrospect it seems that the Patriots' victory was less an upset than a lack of national appreciation for a franchise that was about to win three of four Super Bowls and stake a claim as one of the best teams in NFL history.

And then there was Boston College against Holy Cross on November 28, 1942. Led by running back Mike Holovak, the top-ranked Eagles won their first eight games that season, shut out five teams, and outscored opponents 249-19, including their last six by 168-8. BC was so highly regarded that it entered the regular season finale against 4-4-1 Holy Cross a four-touchdown favorite. After taking care of the rival Crusaders, the Eagles were expected to play Tulsa in the Sugar Bowl for their first national championship.

A crowd of 41,000-plus crammed Fenway Park to watch the Eagles roll, but they instead saw one of the biggest upsets in college history. Holy Cross scored first, halfback Johnny Bezemes rushed for three touchdowns and threw for another, and the Crusaders went on to a 55-12 rout that ended BC's national championship hopes. The Eagles wound up with an Orange Bowl invitation, but lost to

Alabama and finished the season with a No. 8 ranking.

What makes the upset so memorable, however, is not just what happened on the field during the game but what happened afterward. Overly confident that they would beat Holy Cross easily, some Boston College players had reserved a table at the Cocoanut Grove nightclub that night to celebrate the big victory. Depressed by the loss, though, they switched plans and went to the Statler Hotel instead.

While the Eagles consoled themselves at the Statler, the Cocoanut Grove burned in the second-deadliest building fire in U.S. history, killing 492 people. Would the Eagles have been among the victims had they not been upset? "I've been thinking about it all my life," 1942 Eagles player Ed Burns told the *Boston Globe* 50 years later.

WHAT WAS THE MOST EMBARRASSING MOMENT IN BOSTON SPORTS?

97

We mean other than the Red Sox appearance on *Queer Eye for the Straight Guy*.

There was the Boston Massacre in 1978, when the Red Sox lost four consecutive games to the Yankees, were outscored 42-9, and fell out of first place after having held a 12½ game lead. And there was Super Bowl XX, when the Patriots gave up 44 unanswered points, were held to minus 19 yards of offense in the first half, and allowed an offensive lineman to rush for a touchdown in a 46-10 loss. And there was the day the Celtics traded for Vin Baker.

But the most embarrassing moment was when Rosie Ruiz won the 1980 Boston Marathon.

Boston not only is the oldest and grandest marathon in the world, it's the greatest race, period. The Indy 500? The Daytona 500? The Kentucky Derby? The Milwaukee Brewers Sausage Race? Forget it. If you need to sit on top of something else that's doing the work, or you need to turn an ignition switch, then you're just along for the ride. The marathon, however, demands an extraordinary combination of physical and mental conditioning. You can't do it sitting down—you have to run it, all 26.2 grueling miles.

Unless, of course, you're Ruiz.

The Boston Marathon has been run since 1897, never missing a year no matter weather or war. But despite more than a century of races, the most famous moment is also its most infamous. Ask most nonrunners to name a Boston Marathon winner and they probably won't name four-time champ Bill Rodgers or three-time champ Cosmas Ndeti or recordholder Robert Kipkoech Cheruiyot or Alberto Salazar. Instead, they'll name the woman who didn't run it. Ruiz.

Suspicions rose almost immediately after Ruiz crossed the finish line with a winning time of 2:31.56. For one thing, she looked remarkably fresh for someone who had just run 26.2 miles. For another, no one could remember seeing her at any of the checkpoints along the route. For another, some people said they saw her jump onto the course within a half-mile of the finish line. After digging around, race officials also found that Ruiz had qualified for Boston by riding the subway for much of the New York Marathon.

Marathon officials stripped Ruiz of her title and awarded it to Jacqueline Gareau. But despite all the suspicions, all the circumstantial evidence, and all the national punchlines, Ruiz has never admitted to cheating and has also refused to return her first place medal.

But that hasn't kept her from going down in history as the most spectacular cheat in American sports history. Or at least the laziest.

WHO ARE THE MOST INSPIRATIONAL ATHLETES IN BOSTON HISTORY?

How about Tedy Bruschi, for returning to the Patriots less than a year after suffering a stroke? Or how about Curt Schilling for beating the Yankees despite an ankle injury so tender that he was bleeding into his sock when he took the mound?

Hardly. The most inspirational athletes are a 66-year-old ex-Army officer and his 105-pound son, Dick and Rick Hoyt.

When Rick was born, the umbilical cord wrapped around his neck and cut off his air supply. He was brain damaged and left a quadriplegic. He was unable to communicate until he was 11, when engineers at Tufts University developed a computer that allowed him to type with the side of his head. "We were all betting on what his first words would be. 'Hi, Dad' or 'Hi, Mom,'" Dick remembers. "But they were 'Go Bruins.'"

Hey, what can you say? The guy is a Boston fan.

One day, Rick's school held a five-mile run to raise funds for a paralyzed lacrosse player. Rick told his father he wanted to participate and convinced Dick to push his wheelchair the entire five miles. "They took a picture of him when we finished and he had the biggest smile in the world," Dick says. "He wrote me afterward, 'Dad, when we were running, I felt my disability disappear.'"

Well, those words were all it took. A chance to take away his son's disability? Where are the starting lines?

In the nearly three decades since that first five-miler, Dick has pushed and towed Rick in more than 900 competitions. They've competed in the Boston Marathon 25 times (their best time is an astounding 2:40.07) and in Hawaii's Iron Man Triathlon (26.2 mile run, 2.4 mile swim, 112-mile bike ride) six times. They biked and ran across the country in 45 days in 1992-93.

"At every race, we get people coming up to us and saying, 'We used to be on the sidelines but you got us out there,'" Dick says. "I just feel people should get themselves in good shape. They don't have to run marathons and triathlons but they should get out there."

Yeah, it's kind of hard to tell Dick you're too tired or overweight to run when he's training with a 90-pound sack of cement.

Despite doctors' warnings that he would never be able to function and resistance from public schools to admit him, Rick graduated from Boston University. "People with disadvantages should also be included in all physical activities," Dick says. "Rick was always told he can't. Our motto is 'Yes, you can.'"

Dick lives in Holland, Massachusetts, while Rick lives and works in Boston. Dick estimates that if you combine the distances of all the races, the two would have circled the globe three times. Not bad for someone who was told he would never be able to walk on his own.

"Rick's the athlete," Dick says. "I'm just loaning him the arms and legs."

Look, beating the Yankees with a bad ankle is impressive, but try doing it while in a wheelchair—or pushing someone in a wheelchair—the entire game.

ARE THE RED SOX THE NEW YANKEES?

 Prior to the sale of Babe Ruth, the Red Sox were the kings of the American League, the winners of every World Series they ever played and as many as the rest of the AL combined (five).

And then there was a very long drought during which the Red Sox became the symbol of crushing defeat. Mythologized by writers and educators, the Sox were the eternal underdogs, fated to tempt and tease but eventually to lose in the end. "The hero must go under at last," Emily Vermuele wrote of the 1978 playoff, "...To be remembered and immortal and to hear poets sing his tale."

And then the Red Sox finally won a World Series. And it was good.

So now the Red Sox no longer are baseball's perennial underdogs. They are the new Yankees. Consider:

Although the bulk of the outrage gets directed to the Yankees, the Red Sox have had the second highest payroll in the majors for several seasons running. Granted, it's still considerably less than the Yankees', but then again Paul Allen doesn't have as much money as Bill Gates, either. The point is, the two teams spend more money than everyone else.

Heading into the 2006 postseason, the Red Sox still hold the distinction of paying the most money for a world championship (about $127 million). The Yankees certainly have spent more money than that trying to win. Fortunately, at last glance, they hadn't succeeded yet, and the payroll of their most recent championship team was $114 million in 2000.

While the Yankees have the reputation for employing mercenaries, the Red Sox are no better of late. Of the nine players on the field for the final out of the 2004 World Series, not one came up through the Red Sox farm system. The Red Sox' biggest stars in recent years—Manny, Pedro, Papi, Damon, Schilling, Mueller, Millar—all reached Boston via free agency or high-profile trades that were essentially off limits to poorer teams.

Red Sox Nation, meanwhile, has grown so rich and powerful that it deserves a permanent seat on the United

Nations security council. RSN citizens wear Red Sox caps everywhere, Boston's road attendance is exceeded only by the Yankees—Sox fans often outnumber local fans at many road games — and the Sox have the highest average ticket price in baseball by far ($46.46 in 2006). They even charge $30 for standing room only tickets.

Heck, if only John Henry gained 40 pounds and started acting like an ass, you'd think George Steinbrenner owned the team.

For years, Red Sox fans wondered what it would be like to not only win the World Series but to have the talent, the resources, and the attitude to win year after year. Now they do. The Yankees may still be Wal-Mart, but the Red Sox are at least Starbucks.

Feels pretty sweet, doesn't it?

Although, you may not have seen it this way in August and September of 2006.

WHAT'S THE BEST SPORTS COMMERCIAL EVER MADE?

 Aside from talking amphibians and models mud-wrestling in their underwear, nothing better sells a product than a famous athlete. Beer, shoes, deodorant, cars, soda, aftershave, fast food, coffee, financial services, cereal, video games, erectile-dysfunction medicine—if an athlete endorses it, we'll line up at the store to buy it.

We know it doesn't make sense. Just because a guy can take off from the foul line and slam home a two-handed reverse-jam, it doesn't mean we can do the same thing if we buy his brand of shoes. But then again, evidently we also believe that we'll suddenly become very attractive to extremely hot members of the opposite sex if we drink cheap beer (and plenty of it), so it's not that much of a stretch to think that Nike or Adidas can increase our vertical leap by 18 inches.

Not all these advertising pitches work (the Pete Rose Brylcreme commercial springs to mind), but many are so well executed that they leave a longer-lasting impression than the table stains left by our beer bottles while watching the Patriots games. The Mars Blackmon

263

"Gotta Be the Shoes" commercials were the best work Spike Lee had done outside of *Do the Right Thing*, while Bo Jackson's cross-training commercials ("When is that Tour de France thing, anyway?") were better than his actual career.

What's the best commercial featuring an athlete? Many people would pick the Mean Joe Greene commercial, where the lineman gives a kid his jersey in appreciate for being handed a bottle of Coke after a tough game. It's a great commercial, no doubt about it—hell, we still remember it clearly decades later. The problem is, it ruins Mean Joe's reputation. He goes from being one of the NFL's most feared players to a nice guy.

That's not a problem with the best sports commercial—the "Nothing But Net" spot with Larry Bird and Michael Jordan for McDonald's in which the two play a game of H-O-R-S-E to see who buys a Big Mac. The two players start off by sinking a couple easy baskets, then steadily expanding the degree of difficulty until they are banking shots off the scoreboard, over speakers, and even through a window from the parking lot. Eventually they are standing atop the Sears Tower in Chicago talking about a shot bouncing off Michigan Avenue and over the river and hitting . . . nothing but net.

What makes this commercial better than the Mean Joe Greene spot is that it takes the players' reputation as the game's best shooters and playfully enhances it.

The commercial is so clever and fun that the only way to improve it is instead of taking place inside an empty gym, Bird and Jordan are being watched by talking amphibians and models in lingerie.

SOURCES

Most of the research for our arguments came simply from following or covering Boston sports over the past several decades, but several books were very helpful.

Red Sox Century, by Glenn Stout and Richard A. Johnson, is the definitive history of the Red Sox; passionate, balanced–and always thorough.

Rob Neyer's *Book of Baseball Blunders* was especially useful for the argument on Boston's worst managerial moves.

Patrick Sullivan's analysis for *Baseball Prospectus*, "*A WARPed Study of Yankee CF and Red Sox LF*," was very helpful for our argument on the same subject, though we wound up with a somewhat different conclusion.

Other great sources are baseball-reference.com, *The Baseball Encyclopedia, The Sports Encyclopedia of Baseball*, and two wonderful biographies of Ted Williams–*What Do You Think of Ted Williams Now?* by Richard Ben Cramer, and *Ted Williams*, by Leigh Montville.

INDEX
By Subject

269

THE BEST BOSTON SPORTS ARGUMENTS

THE BEST BOSTON SPORTS ARGUMENTS

INDEX
By Name

E

Eagleson, Alan, 180
Eckersley, Dennis, 34
Edmonds, Jim, 87
Elliott, Bob, 90
Ellis, Ed, 145
Elway, John, 113
English, Alex, 243
Epstein, Theo
    "closer by committee" strategy,
      236
    Red Sox 2004 ALCS and, 223–24
    Red Sox 2004 team and, 60–61,
      62, 63
Eruzione, Mike, 205–6, 239
Eshelman, Vaughn, 76
Esposito, Phil, 63–65, 68, 96
Evans, Dwight
    Clemens, Roger, 200
    Hall of Fame and, 67
    as Oriole, 179
    Red Sox 1975 season, 86
    Red Sox 1975 World Series, 202
    Red Sox 1978 season, 34
    Red Sox 1986 season, 86
    Red Sox All-Star Team, 45
Ewing, Patrick, 7

F

Fairbanks, Douglas, 125
Fallon, Jimmy, 60, 242
Fanzone, Carmen, 158–60
Farrelly, Bobby, 158, 242
Farrelly, Peter, 158, 242
Ferguson, John, 220
Fischer, Tom, 144
Fisk, Carlton

All-Star Game (1999), 147
Armbrister, Ed, 177, 178–79
    Fenway Park and, 17
    Good Will Hunting and, 241
    home runs, 57
    Red Sox 1975 season, 86
    Red Sox 1975 World Series, 202,
      249
    Red Sox 1978 season, 34
    Red Sox All-Star Team, 44
    Red Sox front office and, 211,
      212
    uniform number, retired, 31–32
Fitzgerald, Joe, 219
Fitzgerald, Ray, 202
Flutie, Doug, 164
Ford, Eddie, 144
Ford, Harrison, 195
Foster, Otis, 144
Foulke, Keith, 28, 87, 128, 236
Fox, Michael J., 157
Fox, Nellie, 185
Fox, Tim, 141
Foxx, Jimmie, 44
Foy, Joe, 114
Francis, Russ, 209
Francona, Terry, 174
Frazee, Harry, 210
Frazier, Walt, 7
Friday, Bill, 208

G

Gabriele, Dan, 144
Gagliano, Phil, 159
Gaiter, Tony, 145
Galehouse, Denny, 119, 124, 168–69
Gammons, Peter, 102–3, 250

283

289

ABOUT THE AUTHORS

Jim Caple is a senior writer at ESPN.com, with his weekly baseball column "Off Base" for Page 2 among his contributions. Before coming to ESPN, Jim worked in Minneapolis and Seattle. His first book, "The Devil Wears Pinstripes," can also be ordered through his Web site, jimcaple.com.

Steve Buckley has been been a sportswriter for more than 26 years, and has been a columnist with the Boston Herald since 1995. Prior to joining the Herald, he was a columnist for The National Sports Daily, and covered both the Red Sox and the Yankees for The Hartford Courant.

He has written extensively for Boston Magazine, Yankee, The Sporting News and many other magazines. Buckley is a co-host on "The Big Show" on Sportsradio 850 WEEI and also co-hosts a popular Sunday baseball show on the station.

He wrote, produced and directed "I'll Be Seeing You: An American Story of World War II," a television documentary about a war momument located in his native Cambridge, Massachusetts.

Buckley is a co-founder of The Oldtime Baseball Game, an annual charity game featuring top amateur players who wear old-style uniforms from virtually every era in baseball history. The Game has become an annual summertime celebation of baseball in the Boston area.

He is a 1978 graduate of the University of Massachusetts.